OXFORD ILLUSTRATED
SOCIAL STUDIES
DICTIONARY

OXFORD

UNIVERSITY PRESS

OXFORD
UNIVERSITY PRESS

198 Madison Avenue
New York, NY 10016 USA

Great Clarendon Street, Oxford, OX2 6DP,
United Kingdom

Oxford University Press is a department of the University of Oxford. It furthers the University's objective of excellence in research, scholarship, and education by publishing worldwide. Oxford is a registered trade mark of Oxford University Press in the UK and in certain other countries

Library of Congress Cataloging-in-Publication Data

The Oxford illustrated social studies dictionary.
    pages cm
  Audience: Grade 4 to 6
  ISBN 978-0-19-407132-1
1. Social sciences–Dictionaries, Juvenile. I. Oxford University Press. II. Title: Illustrated social studies dictionary. III. Title: Social studies dictionary.
    H41.O94 2013
    300.3–dc23
        2013001019

The moral rights of the author have been asserted

First published in 2013
2017 2016 2015 2014
10 9 8 7 6 5 4 3 2

General Manager: Laura Pearson
Publisher: Stephanie Karras
Managing Editor: Mariel DeKranis
Development Editor: Kelley Perrella
Associate Editor: Rachel Smucker
Director, ADP: Susan Sanguily
Design Manager: Lisa Donovan
Cover Design: Yin Ling Wong
Electronic Production Manager: Julie Armstrong
Designer: Jessica Balaschak
Production Artist: Julie Sussman-Perez
Image Manager: Trisha Masterson
Image Editors: Fran Strauss, Liaht Pashayan, Joe Kassner
Production Coordinator: Brad Tucker

ISBN: 978 0 19 407132 1

Printed in China

This book is printed on paper from certified and well-managed sources

ACKNOWLEDGEMENTS

Illustrations by: Thomas Bayley, Blackwatch Creative, Peter Bull Art Studio, John Edwards, Mike Gardner, Graphic Map & Chart Co., Philip Howe, Bob Kaganich, Karen Minot, Terry Paczko, James Palmer, Julie Sussman-Perez, Ralph Voltz, and John White.

The publishers would like to thank the following for their kind permission to reproduce photographs:

Cover photos: Egyptian/Bridgeman Art Library/Getty Images (mask), various images GmbH & Co.KG/Alamy (coins), Anna Kucherova/shutterstock (quill), David Joyner/istockphoto (Capitol)

pg. 2: Bettmann/CORBIS; pg. 3: Mona Makela/shutterstock, Paul Matthew Photography/shutterstock, Dja65/shutterstock; pg. 4: Elyse Lewin/Photographer's Choice/Getty Images; pg. 6: J.P. MOCZULSKI/AP Photo, 375Ultramag/shutterstock.com, Lintao Zhang/Getty Images News/Getty Images; pg. 7: Richard Drew/AP Photo, David Ball/Alamy; pg. 9: Anonymous/C-RMBett/AP Photo, AFP/Getty Images; pg. 10: Hulton Archive/Stringer/Getty Images, Anonymous/Metropolitan Water District Of Southern California/AP Photo; pg.11: Christine Webb/Alamy, Rechitan Sorin/shutterstock; pg. 12: Michael Benanav/Lonely Planet Images/Getty Images, Everett Collection Inc/Alamy, Collection of the Lowe Art Museum, University of Miami/Gift of George and Julianne Alderman/Bridgeman Art Library; pg. 13: World History Archive/Alamy, Alfred Eisenstaedt/Time & Life Pictures/Getty Images, Warren K. Leffler/http://www.loc.gov/pictures/item/2003688164/Library of Congress, Bettmann/CORBIS, Gideon Mendel/CORBIS; pg.14: Kaetana/shutterstock, Lisa F. Young/istockphoto, The Gallery Collection/CORBIS; pg.15: Pictorial Press Ltd/Alamy; pg. 17: North Wind Picture Archives/Alamy; pg. 18: AES/Domestic News/AP Photo; pg. 19: Eliza Snow/istockphoto; pg. 20: Dennis Donohue/shutterstock, Stocktrek Images, Inc./Alamy; pg. 21: North Wind Picture Archives/Alamy; pg. 22: Everett Collection Inc/Alamy; pg. 23: Luciano Mortula/shutterstock; pg. 24: STF/AP Photo, American School/Private Collection/Peter Newark American Pictures/Bridgeman Art Library, catnap72/istockphoto; pg. 25: B.S.Karan/shutterstock, Proehl Studios/CORBIS, VanHart/shutterstock; pg.26: Monkey Business Images/shutterstock, Henryk Sadura/istockphoto, Dwight Nadig/istockphoto, pagadesign/istockphoto; pg. 27: AP Photo, Dirck Halstead/Time & Life Pictures/Getty Images; pg. 28: Patrick Henry arguing the Parson's Cause at Hanover Courthouse, 1834 (oil on canvas), Cooke, George (1793-1849)/Virginia Historical Society, Richmond, Virginia, USA/The Bridgeman Art Library; pg. 30: Bettmann/CORBIS, Georgi Georgiev/istockphoto; pg.31: Globe Turner, LLC/Getty Images, ZUMA Press, Inc./Alamy; pg. 32: Kaetana/shutterstock, Nataiki/shutterstock; pg.33: Warren K. Leffler/http://www.loc.gov/pictures/item/2003688164/Library of Congress, Frederick Carada/Private Collection/Peter Newark Military Pictures/Bridgeman Art Library; pg. 34: Hulton Archive/Staff/Getty Images, Michael Benanav/Lonely Planet Images/Getty Images; pg.35: sjlocke/istockphoto, Stefano Bianchetti/CORBIS; pg. 36: Shepard Sherbell/CORBIS SABA; pg. 37: pagadesign/istockphoto, FlamingPumpkin/Getty Images, Sports Illustrated/Getty Images; pg. 38: WillSelarep/istockphoto, Frederick Carada/Private Collection/Peter Newark Military Pictures/Bridgeman Art Library; pg. 39: Mark Wilson/Getty Images News/Getty Images, Willierossin/shutterstock, Pictorial Press Ltd/Alamy; pg. 40: Eliza Snow/istockphoto; pg. 41: Classix/istockphoto, Golden Pixels LLC/Alamy; pg. 42: DIZ Muenchen GmbH, Sueddeutsche Zeitung Photo/Alamy; pg. 44: Marli Miller/Visuals Unlimited/CORBIS, Marli Miller/Visuals Unlimited/CORBIS, Chikei Yung/istockphoto, peng wu/istockphoto, hudiemm/istockphoto, timy/shutterstock; pg. 45: malerapaso/istockphoto, Chuck Savage/CORBIS, Classic Image/Alamy; pg. 46: Pictorial Parade/Archive Photos/Getty Images; pg. 47: Lebrecht Music and Arts Photo Library/Alamy, Rich Legg/istockphoto, Aflo Co. Ltd./Alamy; pg. 48: Mark Wilson/Getty Images; pg. 50: Danny Lehman/CORBIS, Popperfoto/Getty Images; pg. 51: AFP/Getty Images/Newscom, Bettmann/CORBIS, Farah Abdi Warsameh/International News/AP Photo; pg. 52: Monkey Business Images/shutterstock, North Wind Picture Archives/Alamy; pg. 53: Everett Collection Inc/Alamy, Everett Collection Historical/Alamy, Scott Olson/Getty Images News/Getty Images, Ocean/CORBIS; pg. 54: michaeljung/shutterstock, Superstock/Masterfile; pg. 55: Jani Bryson/istockphoto, Ingram Publishing/Alamy; pg. 56: Arsgera/istockphoto, MCT/Contributor/McClatchy-Tribune/Getty Images; pg. 57: Paolo Gaetano Rocco/Getty images, Bettmann/CORBIS; pg. 58: Everett Collection Inc/Alamy; pg. 59: Monkey Business Images/

continued on page 218

Contents

How to Read a Dictionary Entry ii

Pronunciation Key iii

Dictionary Entries 2

Word Lists by Social Studies Category 206

Spotlight on Presidents 213

United States Map 214

World Map 216

Acknowledgments

Our National Standards and Social Studies Consultant

Jeff Passe, Ph.D.

Dr. Jeff Passe is Dean of the School of Education at The College of New Jersey. He is a past-President of the National Council for the Social Studies, and was Faculty President and Chair of the Faculty Assembly at the University of North Carolina-Charlotte. He taught elementary school in Gainesville, Florida before earning his doctorate degree in Curriculum and Instruction from the University of Florida.

Dr. Passe has also served as a consultant for several educational and arts organizations throughout North and South Carolina. He has written three elementary-level social studies textbooks and has published articles in more than two dozen professional journals. Most recently, Dr. Passe coordinated the 35-state Survey on the Status of Social Studies.

Each part of the entry helps you learn the term.

Each **entry** is listed in alphabetical order.

The **pronunciation guide** tells you how to say the term. See the Pronunciation Key on page iii to help you.

The **abbreviation** tells you what part of speech the term is. The abbreviations used in the Dictionary are:

- v. (verb)
- n. (noun)
- adj. (adjective)
- abbr. (abbreviation)

capitol /KAP uh tuhl/ (n.)

the building where the laws of each state are made

See also: **capital, government, law, legislation, state**

The Illinois state government meets in the **capitol** in Springfield.

The **definition** tells you the meaning of the term.

The **pictures** and **examples** make the meaning of the term clear and easy to understand.

The box lists **other important terms** in the Dictionary related to the entry. If you see a word you don't know in the definition or the example, look for it in this box.

The **example sentence** uses the term. It helps you understand how to talk about the term.

Vowel Sounds	Like the Sound in . . .	Consonant Sounds	Like the Sound in . . .
a	bat, map	b	boy, job
ay	ate, say	ch	chair, lunch
ah	father, calm	d	day, mud
air	care, fair	f	fall, brief
ar	car, far	g	gone, bug
e	met, step	h	hear, hail
ee	me, equal	j	jaw, enjoy, gel
ur	fern, stir, burn	k	key, cold, took, track
i	if, fit	l	lake, tool
ī	ice, time, fly	m	my, jam
o	stop, clock	n	night, run
oh	ocean, load	ng	song, bring
or	orange, orbit	p	pay, stop
aw	jaw, talk	r	rake, press
oi	soil, boy	s	slow, bus
ow	out, flower	sh	short, bush
uh	cut, summer	t	tip, out
u	full, put	th	thick, bath
oo	soon, prove	TH	there, weather
		v	voice, save
		w	won, winter
		y	yes, young
		z	zoo, freeze
		zh	treasure

Stressed syllables appear in capital letters: /KOL uh nee/

Aa

abolish /uh BOL ish/ (v.)

to put an end to

Abraham Lincoln signed the Emancipation Proclamation to **abolish** slavery.

See also: **civil war; Emancipation Proclamation; freedom; slavery; South, the**

---

absolute location

/AB suh loot loh KAY shun/ (n.)

the exact position of a person, place, or thing on Earth

The **absolute location** of Miami is 25° north and 80° west.

See also: **latitude line, location, longitude line, map, relative location**

A.D. /ay dee/ (abbr.)

used to describe the years since A.D. 1 (also known as C.E.)

2000 B.C.   1000 B.C.   A.D. 1   A.D. 1000   A.D. 2000

Dates with **A.D.** are on the right side of a timeline. Dates with B.C. are on the left.

See also: **age, B.C., era, timeline, time period**

adapt /uh DAPT/ (v.)
to change to fit the environment

See also: **assimilate, immigrant, immigration, pioneer**

Pioneers learned to **adapt** to cold places. They built houses with fireplaces and chimneys.

adobe /uh DOH bee/ (n.)
a type of clay sometimes used to make buildings

See also: **architecture; Native Americans; Southwest, the**

People can make **adobe** into bricks. Buildings made from **adobe** are found in the Southwest.

age /ayj/ (n.)
a particular period in history

See also: **A.D., B.C., era, time period, tool**

The Iron **Age** took place from about 1200 to 1000 B.C. People of the Iron **Age** built metal tools.

agrarian /uh GRAIR ee uhn/ (adj.)
related to farmers and their way of life

See also: **agriculture, economy, farming, rural, society**

The United States was an **agrarian** society in the early 1800s.

agreement /uh GREE muhnt/ (n.)

an understanding reached by two or more people, groups, or nations

See also: **American Revolution, nation, treaty, Treaty of Paris**

The Treaty of Paris was an **agreement** made in 1783 between the United States and Great Britain.

agriculture
/AG ruh kuhl chur/ (n.)

the act of growing food on farms

See also: **agrarian, cash crop, farming, product, rural**

Corn is the main product of U.S. **agriculture**.

allegiance /uh LEE juhns/ (n.)

strong support for one's country

See also: **country, government, nation, patriot, Pledge of Allegiance**

Many Americans say the Pledge of **Allegiance**. This is one way to show support for the United States.

alliance /uh LĪ uhns/ (n.)

a group of countries that
work together

See also: **Allied Powers, ally,
Axis Powers, country, World War II**

The United States, Great Britain, and the U.S.S.R. formed
an **alliance** during World War II.

Allied Powers
/AL īd POW urz/ (n.)

a group of nations that fought
against the Axis Powers
in World War II

World War II Allied Powers

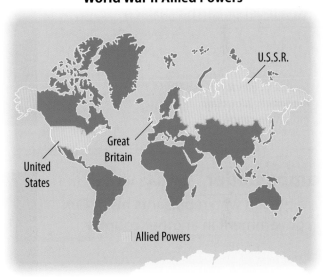

See also: **alliance, ally, Axis Powers,
nation, World War II**

The main **Allied Powers** were the United States,
Great Britain, and the U.S.S.R.

allocate /AL uh kayt/ (v.)

to give a specific share
of resources

School Spending

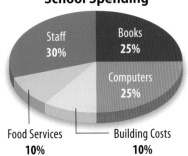

A state government
can **allocate** half
(50%) of school
spending to books
and computers.

See also: **government, limited resource,
natural resource, resource**

ally /AL ī/ (n.)

a country that helps
another country

Canada is an **ally** of the United States.

See also: **alliance, Allied Powers, Axis Powers, country, nation**

altitude /AL tuh tood/ (n.)

the height of something above
sea level or Earth's surface

Mount McKinley has an **altitude** of more than 20,000 feet.

See also: **elevation, landform, landmark, mountain, mountain range**

ambassador /am BAS uh dur/ (n.)

a person who represents his or her
government in another country

Gary Locke became the U.S. **ambassador** to China on August 1, 2011.

See also: **country, diplomat, foreign policy, government, nation**

amendment
/uh MEND muhnt/ (n.)

a change to a law or agreement

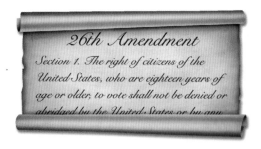

26th Amendment

Section 1. The right of citizens of the United States, who are eighteen years of age or older, to vote shall not be denied or abridged by the United States or by any

See also: **Bill of Rights, Fifteenth Amendment, First Amendment, Fourteenth Amendment, Nineteenth Amendment**

In 1971, the 26th **amendment** to the U.S. Constitution allowed people age 18 and over to vote.

American Revolution
/uh MER uh kuhn rev uh LOO shuhn/ (n.)
(1775–1783)

the war for independence between
Great Britain and the American colonies
(also known as the Revolutionary War)

See also: **colony, Great Britain, independence,
revolution, Revolutionary War**

The 13 colonies won the **American Revolution**
in 1783.

ancestor /AN ses tur/ (n.)

a family member from long ago

See also: **culture, custom, descendant,
generation, tradition**

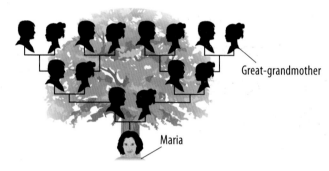

Great-grandmother

Maria

Maria's great-grandmother is her **ancestor**.

ancient /AYN shuhnt/ (adj.)

relating to a time many years
in the past

See also: **age, Ancient Greece,
Ancient Rome, culture, time period**

Ancient Chinese culture
began around 2100 B.C.
Ancient Chinese art can
be seen in museums today.

Ancient Greece
/AYN shuhnt grees/ (n.)
(776 B.C.–323 B.C.)

an early civilization that introduced
the important ideas of philosophy,
architecture, and politics

See also: **Athens, culture, Peloponnesian War,
Sparta, Western civilization**

The first outdoor theaters were built
in **Ancient Greece**.

Ancient Rome
/AYN shuhnt rohm/ (n.)
(c. 753 B.C.–A.D. 476)

an early civilization
with a large empire

See also: **civilization, culture, emperor, Roman Empire, Roman Republic**

Ancient Rome had an empire that covered areas in Europe, Asia, and Africa.

annex /AN eks/ (v.)

to add an area or region
to a country or state

See also: **Congress, country, territorial expansion, territory, vote**

Congress voted to **annex** Texas in 1845. That vote made Texas a part of the United States.

Anthony, Susan B.
/AN thuh nee, SOO zin bee/ (n.)
(1820–1906)

a leader in the movement
for women's right to vote
in the United States

Susan B. Anthony fought for women's suffrage.

See also: **leader, Nineteenth Amendment, suffrage, vote**

Anti-Federalist
/an ti FED ur uh list/ (n.)

a person who did not want the
U.S. Constitution passed

See also: **Bill of Rights, citizen, constitution, federal government, Federalist**

Patrick Henry was
an **Anti-Federalist**.
He argued that the
U.S. Constitution gave
too much power to the
federal government.

Appalachian Mountains
/ap uh LAY chuhn MOWN tuhnz/ (n.)

a large mountain range
in North America

Appalachian
Mountains

See also: **altitude, landform, landmark, mountain, mountain range**

The **Appalachian Mountains** separate the eastern
coast of the United States from the rest of the country.

appoint /uh POINT/ (v.)

to name a person to a position
in government or business

See also: **ambassador, authority, government, justice, president**

The president can **appoint** new justices to the
Supreme Court.

9

Appomattox Court House
/ap uh MAT uhks kort hows/ (n.)

the place in Appomattox, Virginia, where the U.S. Civil War ended

See also: **civil war; North, the; South, the; surrender**

General Robert E. Lee surrendered to General Ulysses S. Grant at the **Appomattox Court House** on April 9, 1865.

apprentice /uh PREN tis/ (n.)

a person who learns a new job

See also: **guild, labor, labor union, manufacturing, trade**

The carpenter's **apprentice** is learning how to make a chair.

aqueduct /AK wuh dukt/ (n.)

a system that moves water a long distance

See also: **canal, irrigation, river, waterway**

An **aqueduct** helps provide water to people who live far from lakes and rivers.

archaeologist
/ar kee OL uh jist/ (n.)

a person who studies humans who lived in the past by looking at tools and household items

See also: **ancient, artifact, civilization, excavate**

An **archaeologist** spends time looking for tools and other artifacts.

architecture /AR kuh tek chur/ (n.)

the style of buildings common in an area or time period

See also: **adobe, Ancient Greece, artifact, pyramid, time period**

Stone buildings with columns are an example of ancient Greek **architecture**.

Arctic /ARK tik/ (n.)

the part of Earth farthest north

See also: **geography, globe, latitude line**

Arctic

Alaska

Canada

The **Arctic** can get very cold. Parts of Canada and Alaska are in the **Arctic**.

armistice /AR muh stis/ (n.)

an agreement to stop or end fighting in a war

See also: **agreement, treaty, World War I**

THE NEWS

VOL.24   Today's Edition   November 11th, 1918

GERMANS SIGN ARMISTICE
WORLD WAR COMES TO END

An **armistice** ended World War I. It was signed on November 11, 1918.

arms race /ARMZ rays/ (n.)

a competition between countries to get the strongest and most weapons

See also: **Cold War, the; compete; competition; conflict; U.S.S.R.**

The United States and the U.S.S.R. were in an **arms race** during the Cold War from 1947 to 1991.

Articles of Confederation
/AR tuh kuhlz uv kuhn fed uh RAY shuhn/ (n.)

the first constitution of the United States

The **Articles of Confederation** was approved in 1781. It created strong state governments.

See also: **American Revolution, constitution, federal government**

artifact /AR tuh fakt/ (n.)

an object made by people in the past

See also: **ancient, archaeologist, culture, product, tool**

Archaeologists study **artifacts**, such as this ancient Chinese cooking pot, to learn how people lived in the past.

assassination
/uh SAS in ay shun/ (n.)

the murder of a leader or
other important person

See also: **civil war, leader, president**

The **assassinations** of President Abraham Lincoln
(left) and President John F. Kennedy (right) shocked
the nation.

---

assembly   /uh SEM blee/ (n.)

a group of people gathered
together for a particular reason

See also: **Bill of Rights, civil rights,
First Amendment, freedom, right**

Americans have freedom of **assembly**. They can
gather to march for their rights.

---

assembly line
/uh SEM blee līn/ (n.)

a system of making goods
cheaply and quickly

See also: **goods, factory, manufacturing,
product, productivity**

Each person does
a different job on
an **assembly line**.

---

assimilate
/uh SIM uh layt/ (v.)

to become more like the culture
around you

See also: **culture, custom, immigrant,
immigration, multicultural**

Children **assimilate** to life in the United States
by learning English.

Athens /ATH uhnz/ (n.)
the capital city of Greece

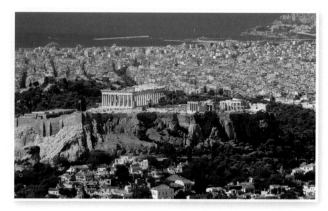

See also: **Ancient Greece, city-state, culture, Peloponnesian War, Sparta**

Athens was a powerful city-state in Ancient Greece. People can still visit the ancient buildings in **Athens**.

authority /uh THOR uh tee/ (n.)
the power to take a specific action

See also: **constitution, government, law, power, president**

The police have the **authority** to arrest a person who breaks the law.

autocrat /AW tuh krat/ (n.)
a person who controls all of the power in a country

In 1804, Napoleon made himself emperor of France. He ruled as an **autocrat**.

See also: **dictator, emperor, power, tyranny**

autonomy /aw TAHN uh mee/ (n.)

the freedom to govern oneself

See also: **American Revolution, constitution, government, independence, self-government**

The United States won **autonomy** from Great Britain after the American Revolution.

Axis Powers /AKS is POW urz/ (n.)

a group of nations that fought against the Allied Powers in World War II

See also: **alliance, Allied Powers, ally, World War II**

World War II Axis Powers

Germany

Italy

Japan

Axis Powers

Germany, Japan, and Italy made up the **Axis Powers**.

Aztec /AZ tek/ (n.)

a group of native people who had a large civilization in Mexico

See also: **civilization, empire, Inca, Maya, Native Americans**

Mexico

■ Aztec Empire, A.D. 1325–1521

The **Aztec** ruled a large empire in central and southern Mexico during the 1400s and 1500s.

Bb

ballot /BAL uht/ (n.)
a card or slip of paper used to vote

Pat Lee and Jim May are both on the **ballot** for class president.

See also: **campaign, candidate, debate, election, vote**

bank /bangk/ (n.)
a business that manages money

See also: **business, financial institution, loan, money**

People keep their money in the **bank**.

barter /BAR tur/ (v.)
to trade one thing for another without using money

See also: **commerce, goods, money, settler, trade**

Native Americans would **barter** furs for tools with settlers.

basin /BAY sin/ (n.)

a low area that drains water from the area around it

Mississippi River Basin

■ Mississippi River Basin

Many rivers flow, or drain, into the Mississippi River **Basin**.

See also: **canal, Mississippi River, river, tributary, waterway**

---

battle /BAT uhl/ (n.)

a fight between enemies

The **Battle** of Gettysburg was fought during the U.S. Civil War.

See also: **civil war, invasion, military, soldier**

B.C. /bee cee/ (abbr.)

used to describe the years before A.D. 1 (also known as B.C.E.)

B.C.

2000 B.C.   1000 B.C.   A.D. 1   A.D. 1000   A.D. 2000

See also: **A.D., age, era, timeline, time period**

Dates with **B.C.** are on the left side of a timeline. Dates with A.D. are on the right.

17

Bell, Alexander Graham
/bel, al ig ZAN dur gram/ (n.)
(1847–1922)

the inventor of many machines, including the telephone

See also: **communication, entrepreneur, impact, innovation, invention**

Alexander Graham Bell invented the telephone in 1876.

---

benefit /BEN uh fit/ (n.)

a payment the government makes to its citizens

See also: **citizen, Congress, government, Senate, Social Security**

The U.S. Social Security program pays money to people age 65 years and older. Social Security is a **benefit**.

Berlin Wall /bur LIN wahl/ (n.)

a wall that divided the German city of Berlin from 1961 to 1989

See also: **border; city; Cold War, the; communism; government**

The **Berlin Wall** once divided East Berlin from West Berlin. The wall was a symbol of the Cold War.

---

bias /BĪ uhs/ (n.)

a strong feeling in favor of or against one group of people

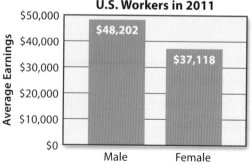

Average Earnings for Full-time U.S. Workers in 2011

Average Earnings

Male: $48,202
Female: $37,118

See also: **discrimination, Jim Crow laws, prejudice, racism, workforce**

In the United States, men earn more money than women for doing the same work. There is a **bias** against women in the workforce.

bill /bil/ (n.)

a draft of a law that has not yet been passed

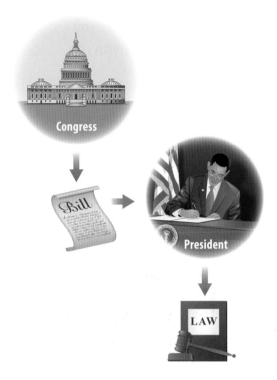

Congress

Bill

President

LAW

See also: **Congress, law, legislation, president, veto**

First, Congress approves a **bill**. Next, the president signs the **bill**. Then it becomes a law.

Bill of Rights /bil uv RĪTS/ (n.)

the first ten amendments to the U.S. Constitution

See also: **amendment, Anti-Federalist, constitution, Federalist, freedom**

The **Bill of Rights** protects the rights and freedoms of all U.S. citizens.

biography /bī OG ruh fee/ (n.)
the life story of a real person

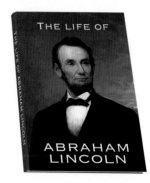

A **biography** gives information about a person's life.

See also: **chronology, history, impact, secondary source**

blockade /blo KAYD/ (n.)
the act of closing off an area

See also: **battle, harbor, invasion, military**

A navy can put a **blockade** around a harbor to keep enemies out.

body of water
/BOD ee uv WAW tur/ (n.)
an area covered by water, such as a lake or a river

See also: **canal, ocean, river, tributary, waterway**

Lake George in New York is a **body of water**.

bond /bond/ (n.)
a loan to be paid back later

A government might sell a **bond** during wartime. People buy the **bond** to help pay for the war.

See also: **debt, economy, loan, money**

border /BOR dur/ (n.)

the imaginary line that divides two pieces of land

See also: **boundary, country, demarcation line, map, state**

The **border** between the United States and Mexico is almost 2,000 miles long.

Boston Massacre
/BAW stuhn MAS uh kur/ (n.)

the killing of five colonists by British soldiers in 1770

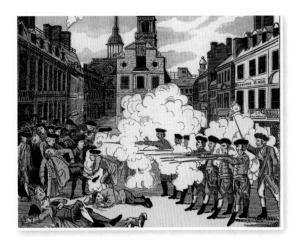

See also: **American Revolution, Boston Tea Party, colony, Great Britain, Revolutionary War**

The **Boston Massacre** helped to start the American Revolution.

Boston Tea Party
/BAW stuhn TEE par tee/ (n.)

a protest by Americans against a British tax on tea

See also: **American Revolution, colony, Great Britain, Revolutionary War, tax**

During the **Boston Tea Party** of 1773, colonists threw tea into Boston Harbor to protest.

boundary /BOWN dree/ (n.)

the edge or end of a country, state, or natural feature

See also: **border, country, geography, map, ocean**

The Atlantic Ocean and the Pacific Ocean each form a natural **boundary** for the United States.

---

branch of government
/BRANCH uv GUHV urn muhnt/ (n.)

a main part of a government

Three Branches of Government

Legislative	Executive	Judicial
Congress	President	Courts

See also: **checks and balances, Congress, president, separation of powers, Supreme Court**

The executive **branch of government** is one of the three branches of the U.S. government.

Brown v. Board of Education
/brown VUR sus bord uv ej uh KAY shuhn/ (n.)

a Supreme Court case in 1954 that made school segregation illegal

See also: **integration, *Plessy v. Ferguson*, racism, segregation, Supreme Court**

Brown v. Board of Education allowed African American students to go to the same school as white students.

Buddhism /BOO diz uhm/ (n.)

a major religion common
in parts of Asia

See also: **Christianity, Hinduism, Islam, Judaism, Shinto**

The eight-spoked wheel, or dharma wheel, is one of the oldest symbols of **Buddhism**.

budget /BUJ it/ (n.)

a plan about how much money
will be made and how it will
be spent

A **budget** can
show how
much money a
person needs
each month.

See also: **debt, expense, income, money**

business /BIZ nis/ (n.)

a company that sells goods
or services

See also: **capitalism, commerce, consumer, goods, money**

A grocery store is a **business** that sells food
and other items.

Cc

Cabinet /KAB uh net/ (n.)

a group of department leaders that helps the president make decisions

See also: **federal government, leader, president**

The Secretary of Education is part of the U.S. president's **Cabinet**. He or she helps the president make decisions on education.

campaign /kam PAYN/ (n.)

a plan to win an election

Workers put up millions of posters during John F. Kennedy's **campaign** for president in 1960.

See also: **candidate, competition, debate, election, vote**

canal /kuh NAL/ (n.)

a waterway built for boats

See also: **goods, irrigation, river, transportation, waterway**

The Erie **Canal** made travel between the Great Lakes and New York City much easier.

candidate /KAN duh dayt/ (n.)

a person who works to win an election

See also: **campaign, competition, election, vote, public service**

A **candidate** makes speeches to share his or her goals for the future.

canyon /KAN yuhn/ (n.)

deep, low land between mountains or hills that has steep sides of rock

Some parts of the Grand **Canyon** are a mile deep.

See also: **geography, landform, mountain, mountain range, physical feature**

cape /kayp/ (n.)

a strip of land that extends into a body of water

See also: **body of water, geography, landform, ocean, peninsula**

Cape Cod is a **cape** that extends into the Atlantic Ocean.

capital /KAP uh tuhl/ (n.)

a city where a country or state government is located

Washington, D.C. is the **capital** of the United States.

See also: **capitol, city, government, state**

capitalism
/**KAP uh tuh liz uhm**/ (n.)

an economy in which businesses are owned by individuals or groups, not the government

See also: **business, consumer, free enterprise, investment, market economy**

Capitalism allows businesses to be owned by citizens.

capitol /**KAP uh tuhl**/ (n.)

the building where the laws of each state are made

See also: **capital, government, law, legislation, state**

The Illinois state government meets in the **capitol** in Springfield.

Capitol, the
/**KAP uh tuhl, тнuh**/ (n.)

the building in Washington, D.C. where Congress meets

See also: **Congress, government, House of Representatives, Senate**

Congress has been meeting at **the Capitol** in Washington, D.C. for over 200 years.

cardinal direction
/**KARD uhn uhl duh REK shuhn**/ (n.)

one of four main directions on a compass

See also: **compass, compass rose, geography, intermediate direction, map**

The four **cardinal directions** on a compass are north, south, east, and west.

Carver, George Washington
/KAR vur, jorj WAHSH ing tuhn/ (n.)
(1861–1943)

an African American scientist
and inventor

See also: **agriculture, crop rotation, impact, innovation, invention**

George Washington Carver invented a method of crop rotation that helped improve farming.

cash crop /kash krop/ (n.)

a plant product grown
by a farmer to be sold
for money

Corn is an important **cash crop** in the United States.

See also: **agriculture, consumer, crop, farming, market economy**

caucus /KAW kuhs/ (n.)

a meeting of members
of a political party

Some states will have a **caucus** to choose their politicians.

See also: **candidate, election, politics, political party, vote**

27

census /SEN suhs/ (n.)

a count taken every 10 years of all the people who live in a country

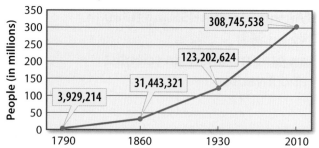

U.S. Population Growth from 1790 to 2010

308,745,538

123,202,624

31,443,321

3,929,214

See also: **country, decade, demographic, population**

The first U.S. **census** in 1790 counted almost four million people. The last U.S. **census** in 2010 counted over 300 million people.

Central America
/SEN truhl uh MER uh kuh/ (n.)

a section of North America that connects North America to South America

Belize

Guatemala

Honduras

Nicaragua

El Salvador

Panama

Costa Rica

See also: **country, culture, globe, map, Maya**

There are seven countries in **Central America**.

central government
/SEN truhl GUHV urn muhnt / (n.)

the group of people that leads a country and its states

See also: **American Revolution, Anti-Federalist, Articles of Confederation, federal government, government**

After the American Revolution, many leaders wanted strong state governments instead of a strong **central government**.

Central Powers
/SEN truhl POW urz/ (n.)

a group of nations who fought against the Allies in World War I

World War I Central Powers

The main **Central Powers** included Germany, Austria-Hungary, Bulgaria, and the Ottoman Empire.

See also: **alliance, ally, World War I**

---

century /SEN chur ee/ (n.)

a period of 100 years

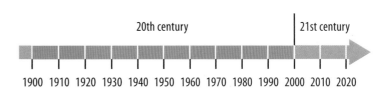

See also: **A.D., age, B.C., era, millennium**

The 20th **century** ended on the last day of the year 2000.

---

checks and balances
/cheks end BAL uhns iz/ (n.)

the way in which each part of the government has some power over the others

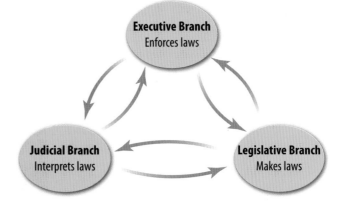

See also: **branch of government, constitution, separation of powers**

The U.S. Constitution has a system of **checks and balances** between branches of government.

29

Chief Justice
/cheef JUHS tis/ (n.)

the justice who is in charge
of the U.S. Supreme Court

William H. Rehnquist
was **Chief Justice** of the
Supreme Court for more
than 18 years.

See also: **constitution, court,
jury, justice, Supreme Court**

Christianity
/kris chee AN uh tee/ (n.)

the beliefs and practices that follow
the teachings of Jesus Christ

See also: **church, monotheism,
mosque, religion, temple**

Christianity has about 2 billion followers
throughout the world. A cross represents
Christianity.

chronology
/kruh NOL uh jee/ (n.)

the order in which
events happen

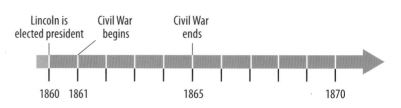

Lincoln is
elected president

Civil War
begins

Civil War
ends

1860 1861   1865   1870

See also: **A.D., B.C., era,
timeline, time period**

A timeline can show the **chronology** of
major events.

church /church/ (n.)
a place of worship for Christians

Many **churches** have
windows made of
stained glass.

See also: **Christianity, monotheism,
mosque, religion, temple**

citizen /SIT uh zuhn/ (n.)

a person who is born in a country
or becomes a member of that
country by law

See also: **constitution, country,
immigrant, immigration, naturalization**

More than 600,000 people become U.S. **citizens**
each year.

city /SIT ee/ (n.)

a place where many people live

See also: **city council, mayor,
metropolitan area, suburb, urban**

Pittsburgh is a large **city** in the state of Pennsylvania.

city council
/SIT ee KOWN suhl/ (n.)

a group of people who
make laws in a city

See also: **city, government, law,
legislation, public service**

A **city council** is part of local government. It can
pass laws on schools, safety, and budget.

31

city-state /SIT ee stayt/ (n.)

a land that ruled itself and
the area around it

See also: **Ancient Greece, Athens,
city, government, nation-state**

Athens was the largest **city-state** in Ancient Greece.

civic participation
/SIV ik par TIS uh pay shuhn/ (n.)

the set of actions taken
by a responsible person
in a city, state, or country

See also: **citizen, responsibility,
volunteer, vote**

To vote is an example of **civic participation**.

civilization
/siv uh luh ZAY shuhn/ (n.)

a culture or society

See also: **city, culture, Maya,
population, society**

The Maya **civilization** built more than 40 large cities
from A.D. 250 to A.D. 900.

civil rights /SIV uhl rīts/ (n.)
the rights that all people
in a society have

See also: **amendment, citizen, civic participation, constitution, society**

Americans have freedom of speech and the right to gather in public. These **civil rights** are protected by the U.S. Constitution.

civil war /SIV uhl wor/ (n.)
a war between people
of the same country

See also: **conflict; North, the; Reconstruction; slavery; South, the**

The U.S. **Civil War** was a fight between the North and South from 1861 to 1865.

coast /kohst/ (n.)
the edge of land along the sea

Boston

The city of Boston is on the northeastern **coast** of the United States.

See also: **body of water, coastal plain, geography, ocean, plain**

33

coastal plain
/KOH stuhl playn/ (n.)

an area of flat land that lies
next to a coast

See also: **body of water, coast, geography, ocean, plain**

Jamestown settlers built homes along the
coastal plain of what is now Virginia.

Cold War, the
/kohld wor, THuh/ (n.)
(1947–1991)

a period of unfriendly but non-
violent relations between the
U.S.S.R. and the United States

See also: **arms race, communism, compete, conflict, democracy**

The U.S.S.R. and the United States competed
in an arms race during **the Cold War**.

colony   /KOL uh nee/ (n.)

a place that is ruled
by another country

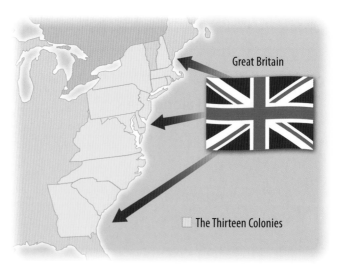

Great Britain

The Thirteen Colonies

See also: **American Revolution, empire, Great Britain, Revolutionary War, settlement**

America was a **colony** of Britain until it won the
American Revolution in 1783.

Columbus, Christopher
/kuh LUM buhs, KRIS tuh fur/ (n.)
(1451–1506)

an Italian explorer who was one of the first Europeans to sail to the Americas

See also: **conquistador, expedition, explore, gold, Native Americans**

Christopher Columbus landed in the Americas on October 12, 1492.

---

commerce /KOM urs/ (n.)
the buying and selling of goods

See also: **economy, free enterprise, goods, market economy, supply and demand**

A farmer's market is a place of **commerce**. People buy and sell fruits and vegetables.

---

common /KOM uhn/ (adj.)
belonging to or shared by members of a group, community, or country

See also: **community, country, nation, suffrage**

These women shared the **common** belief that they should be able to vote.

35

communication
/kuh myoo nuh KAY shuhn/ (n.)

the use of words, sounds, or signs to share information or ideas with other people

See also: **Bell, Alexander Graham; innovation; invention; negotiation**

Computers help to make **communication** easier and faster.

communism
/KOM yuh niz uhm/ (n.)

an economy in which businesses are owned and controlled by the government

See also: **capitalism, compete, democracy, society, U.S.S.R.**

Communism allows only the government to control businesses. The U.S.S.R. economy was an example of **communism**.

community
/kuh MYOO nuh tee/ (n.)

a place where people live and work

See also: **city, city council, civic participation, local, society**

A **community** has libraries, schools, and stores.

compass /KUM puhs/ (n.)

a tool that is used to show direction

A **compass** will always point to the North Pole.

See also: **cardinal direction, compass rose, geography, intermediate direction, map**

---

compass rose
/KUM puhs rohz/ (n.)

a figure on a compass or map that is used to show the cardinal directions

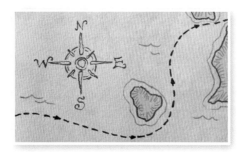

See also: **cardinal direction, compass, geography, intermediate direction, map**

A **compass rose** shows the directions: north, south, east, and west.

---

compete /kum PEET/ (v.)

to try to win a competition

See also: **arms race, business, commerce, competition, product**

Stores **compete** with one another by lowering their prices to win customers.

---

competition
/kom puh TISH uhn/ (n.)

a contest between people, groups, or countries

See also: **arms race; Cold War, the; commerce; compete**

The World Cup is a soccer **competition** between countries around the world.

compromise /KOM pruh mīz/ (n.)

a type of agreement made between people or nations

See also: **agreement, conflict, negotiation, trade-off, treaty**

When people make a **compromise**, they get a part, but not all, of what they want.

Confederacy
/kuhn FED ur uh see/ (n.)

a group of states that left the Union from 1861–1865

See also: **civil war, Continental Army, Reconstruction, secede, slavery**

Eleven states made up the **Confederacy**. The **Confederacy** had its own flag.

conflict /KON flikt/ (n.)

a fight, battle, or war between two sides

See also: **agreement, battle, civil war, states' rights, treaty**

The U.S. Civil War was a **conflict** over slavery and state rights.

Confucianism
/kuhn FYOO shuh niz uhm/ (n.)

a set of beliefs that are based on the ideas of the Chinese teacher Confucius

See also: **community, Confucius**

Confucianism began in China around 500 B.C.

Confucius /kuhn FYOO shuhs/ (n.)
(551 B.C.–479 B.C.)

a famous teacher from China

See also: **Confucianism, education**

Chinese culture was influenced by the teachings of **Confucius.**

Congress /KONG gris/ (n.)

the part of the United States government that makes laws

See also: **branch of government, checks and balances, House of Representatives, representative, Senate**

The Senate and House of Representatives make up the U.S. **Congress**.

conquistador
/kon KEE stuh dor/ (n.)

a Spanish soldier who took new lands by force in the 1500s

Conquistadors came to the Americas in 1519.

See also: **Columbus, Christopher; expedition; explore; Native Americans**

consequence
/KON suh kwens/ (n.)

the result of an action

Damage to buildings and homes is a **consequence** of war.

See also: **conflict, cost, impact**

constitution
/kon stuh TOO shuhn/ (n.)

the system of laws that a country is governed by

See also: **Articles of Confederation, Bill of Rights, citizen, country, law**

The U.S. **Constitution** includes a Bill of Rights to protect the rights of citizens.

consumer /kuhn SOO mur/ (n.)

a person who buys goods or services

See also: **credit, goods, market economy, product, service**

Consumers can go to the store to buy new televisions.

continent /KON tuh nent/ (n.)

one of Earth's seven major bodies of land

See also: **body of water, Eurasia, geography, globe, map**

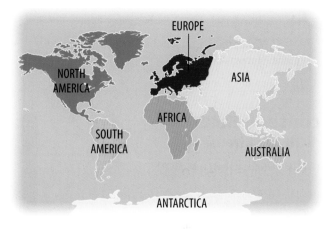

The largest **continent** is Asia. The smallest **continent** is Australia.

Continental Army
/kon tuh NEN tuhl AR mee/ (n.)

the group of Americans that fought in the Revolutionary War

See also: **American Revolution, colony, Declaration of Independence, Great Britain, Revolutionary War**

George Washington led the **Continental Army** against the British army.

Continental Divide
/kon tuh NEN tuhl duh VĪD/ (n.)

a line of mountains in the United States where rivers begin to flow in opposite directions

The **Continental Divide** is in the Rocky Mountains. It runs through five different states.

See also: **body of water, continent, mountain, river, Rocky Mountains**

---

cost /kawst/ (n.)

the money paid or charged for goods or services

The **cost** of the carrots is $1.50 per pound.

See also: **business, commerce, goods, product, service**

---

cotton gin /KOT uhn jin/ (n.)

a machine used to take the seeds out of cotton

The **cotton gin** was important to the cotton industry in the South.

See also: **cash crop; industry; invention; South, the**

country /KUN tree/ (n.)
a land and people
with its own government

See also: **city, city-state, continent, nation, region**

The United States is a **country** in North America.

county /KOWN tee/ (n.)
one of the parts into which
a state is divided

Palm
Beach

See also: **community, country, local, region, state**

Palm Beach is the largest **county** of the 67
counties in Florida.

coup /koo/ (n.)
the act of a small group taking
over a government, usually
by force

See also: **battle, conflict, government, revolution**

The October Revolution was a **coup** in Russia in 1917.

court /kort/ (n.)

a place where a judge or a jury make legal decisions

See also: **defendant, judge, jury, justice, plaintiff**

People go to **court** when they have legal disagreements.

credit /KRED it/ (n.)

a way to buy something and pay for it later

Credit Card Statement

Purchase of TV at **TVs & More: $1,000**

Monthly payment due: **$100**

Due date: **8/27**

See also: **commerce, currency, debt, interest, market economy**

A person can buy a television on **credit** and pay a small amount each month.

crop /krop/ (n.)

a group of plants grown for food

Corn is a common food **crop** in the United States.

See also: **agriculture, cash crop, farming, irrigation**

crop rotation
/krop roh TAY shuhn/ (n.)

a way of planting a different crop each year on the same soil

See also: **agriculture; Carver, George Washington; cash crop; crop; farming**

Crop rotation helps keep the soil healthy for a long time. Farmers will plant lettuce one year and beans the next.

culture /KUL chur/ (n.)

the way of life of a group of people

Clothing and Music

Food

Art

Language

See also: **civilization, community, custom, society, tradition**

Culture includes the food, clothing, music, art, and language of a people.

currency /KUR uhn see/ (n.)

the type of money a country uses

See also: **business, commerce, economy, money**

The dollar is the official **currency** of the United States.

current /KUR uhnt/ (adj.)

happening or being done now

See also: **history, media, predict, trend**

New York, NY

Today's weather

72°
Cloudy

The **current** weather in New York is 72°F and cloudy.

custom /KUS tuhm/ (n.)

the special way a group of people does something

See also: **civilization, culture, history, society, tradition**

Eating turkey at Thanksgiving is a U.S. **custom**.

czar /zar/ (n.)

the title of the ruler of Russia before 1917

See also: **leader, monarchy, oligarchy, power**

The last **czar** of Russia was Nicholas II.

Dd

debate /di BAYT/ (n.)

a discussion in which two or more people give their different opinions on issues

See also: **campaign, candidate, election, issue, president**

John F. Kennedy and Richard Nixon had a presidential **debate** in 1960.

debt /det/ (n.)

the money a person, company, or country owes to another

See also: **bank, credit, expense, income, money**

Credit Card Statement
Purchase of TV at **TVs & More**: **$1,000**
Monthly payment due: **$100**
Due date: **8/27**

Mary used her credit card to buy a new television. She has a **debt** of $1,000.

decade /DEK ayd/ (n.)

a time period of ten years

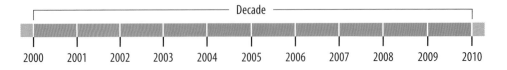

Decade

2000 2001 2002 2003 2004 2005 2006 2007 2008 2009 2010

See also: **century, era, millenium, timeline, time period**

The years between 2000 and 2010 make up a **decade**.

Declaration of Independence
/dek luh RAY shun uv
in di PEN duhns/ (n.)

a document that stated the
American colonies were free
from Great Britain

See also: **American Revolution, autonomy, colony, freedom, Great Britain**

The **Declaration of Independence** was written
by the American colonists. It was approved
on July 4, 1776.

---

defendant   /dee FEN duhnt/ (n.)

a person who is blamed
for a crime

See also: **judge, jury, justice, law, plaintiff**

The judge found the **defendant** guilty of the crime.

---

defense   /di FENS/ (n.)

the protection of someone
or something

See also: **country, military, soldier, terrorism**

The U.S. Department of **Defense** protects the
country. The Navy is a part of the Department
of **Defense**.

47

deficit /DEF uh sit/ (n.)

an amount of money that is less than the amount of money needed

See also: **bank, Congress, cost, debt, expense**

Congress meets to decide how to lower the **deficit**.

deflation /di FLAY shun/ (n.)

a decrease in available money that causes prices to go down

See also: **cost, currency, inflation, money, surplus**

Having too much of one product can cause a **deflation** in prices.

demand /di MAND/ (n.)

how much a product or service is needed or wanted

See also: **goods, price, product, service, supply and demand**

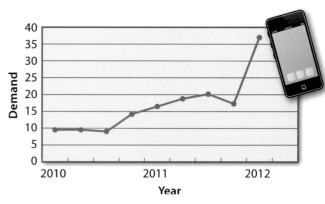

The **demand** for a popular smartphone increased from 8 million in 2010 to over 35 million in 2012.

demarcation line
/dee mar KAY shun līn/ (n.)

a boundary that separates two countries

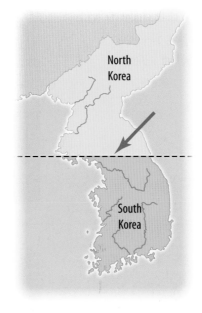

The **demarcation line** between North Korea and South Korea was set in 1953 after the Korean Conflict.

See also: **border, boundary, Korean Conflict, region**

---

democracy   /di MOK ruh SEE/ (n.)

a form of government in which the leader or leaders are chosen by the people in an election

See also: **citizen, election, representative, right, vote**

The United States is a **democracy**. U.S. citizens have the right to vote for their representatives.

---

demographic
/dem uh GRAF ik/ (n.)

a specific detail that identifies a group of people

PBS NewsHour Audience (by age)

Under 25

25–54

55+

See also: **census, community, consumer, income, population**

The major **demographic** for PBS NewsHour, a popular news show in the United States, is people age 55 and over.

49

descendant /di SEN duhnt/ (n.)

a person who comes from a
group of people who lived
a long time ago

This girl is a
descendant of the
ancient Maya people.

See also: **ancestor, culture,
generation, Maya**

development
/di VEL uhp muhnt/ (n.)

the act of making an
economy stronger

See also: **community, economy, expansion,
impact, transportation**

Economic **development** includes building new
schools, roads, and businesses.

dictator /DIK tay tur/ (n.)

a ruler with complete power who
often rules in an unfair way

Adolf Hitler (left) was the **dictator** of Germany
from 1933 to 1945. Benito Mussolini (right) was
the **dictator** of Italy from 1922 to 1943.

See also: **fascism; Hitler, Adolf;
leader; power; World War II**

diplomat   /DIP luh mat/ (n.)

a person who represents his or her government when dealing with other governments

Susan E. Rice is an American **diplomat**.

See also: **ambassador, country, foreign policy, government, negotiation**

discrimination

/dis krim uh NAY shuhn/ (n.)

the act of treating a person or group unfairly because of race, religion, or gender

The Jim Crow laws allowed for **discrimination** against African Americans.

See also: **civil rights, ethnicity, Jim Crow laws, prejudice, racism**

displace   /dis PLAYS/ (v.)

to make people leave their home or country

A famine can **displace** many families from their homeland.

See also: **country, famine, homeland, refugee**

distribution

/dis truh BYOO shuhn/ (n.)

the delivery of goods or
resources to many people

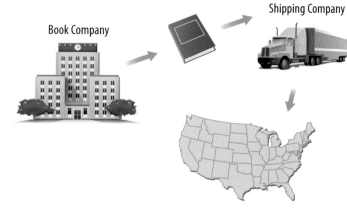

Book Company

Shipping Company

See also: **business, commerce,
goods, resource, service**

Shipping companies handle the **distribution** of books
to stores all over the United States.

diversity /di VUR suh tee/ (n.)

a variety of people from different
backgrounds in a group

See also: **culture, demographic,
ethnicity, multicultural**

New students from different countries help
increase **diversity** in U.S. schools.

Douglass, Frederick

/DUG luhs, FRED ur ik/ (n.)
(1818–1895)

a former slave who became
a human-rights leader
in the United States

Frederick Douglass
wrote about his life
as a slave. He helped
turn many people
against slavery.

See also: **abolish, equality,
Emancipation Proclamation,
slave, slavery**

Dred Scott v. Sandford
/dred skot VUR sus SAND ford/ (n.)

a Supreme Court ruling in 1857 that stated slaves were not U.S. citizens and that slavery was legal

NOW READY:
THE
Dred Scott Decision.
OPINION OF CHIEF-JUSTICE
ROGER B. TANEY.
WITH AN INTRODUCTION,
BY DR. J. H. VAN EVRIE.
ALSO,
By SAM. A. CARTWRIGHT, M.D., of New Orleans,
ENTITLED,
"Natural History of the Prognathous
Race of Mankind."
ORIGINALLY WRITTEN FOR THE NEW YORK DAY-BOOK.

Dred Scott

See also: **citizen, equality, legal, slavery, Supreme Court**

Dred Scott was a slave who went to court to fight for his freedom. The decision of *Dred Scott v. Sandford* angered people who were against slavery.

---

drought /drowt/ (n.)

a long time period with little or no rain

See also: **agriculture, crop, farming, time period**

The **drought** in 2011 in Texas caused many crops to die.

---

due process /doo PROS es/ (n.)

a citizen's right to be treated fairly

The right to a public trial is part of the **due process** for anyone accused of a crime.

See also: **constitution, legal, prosecutor, right, trial**

earnings /UR ningz/ (n.)

the money or profit made
by working

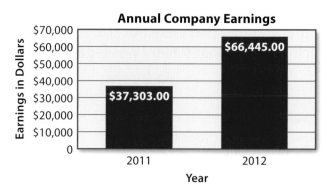

Annual Company Earnings

Earnings in Dollars

$70,000
$60,000
$50,000
$40,000
$30,000
$20,000
$10,000
0

$37,303.00

$66,445.00

2011   2012

Year

See also: **currency, income,
income tax, money, workforce**

The **earnings** of the company increased in 2012.

economy /i KON uh mee/ (n.)

a country's system for managing
its resources and businesses

See also: **currency, money,
recession, resource**

People spend more money when the **economy**
is healthy.

Edison, Thomas
/ED uh suhn, TOM uhs/ (n.)
(1847–1931)

an American inventor and
businessman

Thomas Edison
invented the light bulb.

See also: **business, entrepreneur,
innovation, invention, manufacturing**

education /ej uh KAY shuhn/ (n.)

the process of teaching
and learning

See also: *Brown v. Board of Education,*
civil rights, communication, integration,
Plessy v. Ferguson

More than 75 million children and adults in the
United States received an **education** in 2009.

election /i LEK shuhn/ (n.)

a time when people vote
for their leaders

See also: **ballot, candidate, democracy,**
president, vote

Elections allow citizens to choose their leaders.

Electoral College
/i LEK tur uhl KOL ij/ (n.)

a group of people chosen
to elect the U.S. president
based on how the people
in each state voted

Electoral College Votes, 2012

See also: **constitution, democracy,**
election, president, vote

California has the most **Electoral College** votes
because it has the largest population.

55

elevation /el uh VAY shuhn/ (n.)

the height of a place above sea level or the Earth's surface

See also: **altitude, geography, mesa, mountain, mountain range**

Mt. Everest has the highest **elevation** above sea level.

Emancipation Proclamation
/i man suh PAY shuhn prok luh MAY shuhn/ (n.)

a document signed in 1863 by President Abraham Lincoln that freed the slaves in the Confederacy

See also: **civil war; Confederacy; president; slave; Union, the**

Nearly 180,000 freed slaves joined the Union Army after the **Emancipation Proclamation** was issued.

embargo /em BAR goh/ (n.)

a government rule that prevents trade with a specific country

See also: **commerce, conflict, government, petroleum, trade**

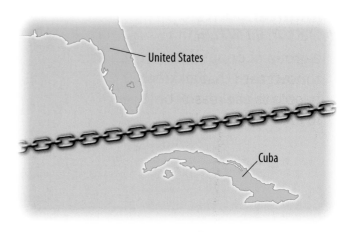

United States

Cuba

The United States has had a trade **embargo** against Cuba since January, 1961.

emperor /EM pur ur/ (n.)

a man who rules an empire

Augustus was the first **emperor** of the Roman Empire. He ruled from 27 B.C. to A.D. 14.

See also: **empire, government, leader, monarchy, Roman Empire**

empire /EM pīr/ (n.)

a group of countries or regions ruled by one person or government

Atlantic Ocean
ASIA
EUROPE
Black Sea
Rome
Mediterranean Sea
AFRICA
■ Roman Empire, A.D. 14

See also: **Aztec, emperor, leader, Ottoman Empire, Roman Empire**

The Roman **Empire** was established in 27 B.C. The **empire** included Greece, Egypt, and many other lands.

Enlightenment
/en LĪT en muhnt/ (n.)
(1600s–1700s)

a movement that challenged people to use reason and science to look at the world

During the **Enlightenment**, people such as Isaac Newton made many scientific discoveries.

See also: **age, invention, movement, religion**

57

entrepreneur
/ahn truh pruh NUR/ (n.)

a person who takes the risk of starting a new business

See also: **budget, business, economy, money, risk**

In 2009, businesses started by **entrepreneurs** created 2.3 million new jobs in the United States.

equality /i KWOL uh tee/ (n.)

the condition of having the same rights as everyone else

See also: *Brown v. Board of Education;* civil rights; King, Jr., Dr. Martin Luther; Parks, Rosa

African Americans fought for **equality** in schools during the U.S. Civil Rights movement.

era /ER uh/ (n.)

a period of time usually marked by an important event or person

See also: **A.D., age, timeline, time period**

The Victorian **Era** was named after Queen Victoria. She ruled Great Britain from 1837 to 1901.

ethnicity /eth NI suh tee/ (n.)
a group of people who share the same culture and history

See also: **civil rights, culture, diversity, history, multicultural**

There are children of many different **ethnicities** in U.S. schools.

Eurasia /yur AY zhuh/ (n.)
a land mass that includes Europe and Asia

See also: **continent, geography, globe, map, population**

Eurasia

Over 70% of the Earth's population (over 4.6 billion people) live in **Eurasia**.

evidence /EV uh duhns/ (n.)
information that proves something is real or true

See also: **defendant, justice, law, legal, prosecutor**

The detective found **evidence** of the thief's fingerprints at the crime scene.

excavate /EK skuh vayt/ (v.)
to dig up and take out

See also: **ancient, Ancient Greece, archaeologist, artifact, culture**

Archaeologists **excavate** objects that have been buried for a long time.

exchange /eks CHAYNJ/ (v.)

to give or receive something
in return for something else

Early American settlers **exchanged** tools for food
and furs with Native Americans.

See also: **barter, money,
settler, trade**

expansion /ek SPAN shuhn/ (n.)

the act of increasing in size

See also: **expedition, Lewis and Clark,
Louisiana Purchase, territorial expansion,
territory**

The Louisiana Purchase in 1803 led to a large
expansion of the United States.

expedition
/ek spuh DISH uhn/ (n.)

a journey made
for a specific reason

← Route taken by
Lewis and Clark in 1804

See also: **Columbus, Christopher;
conquistador; explore; Lewis and Clark;
Louisiana Purchase**

Lewis and Clark led an **expedition** in 1804 to study
the new land purchased by the United States.

expense /ek SPENS/ (n.)

money spent to buy something

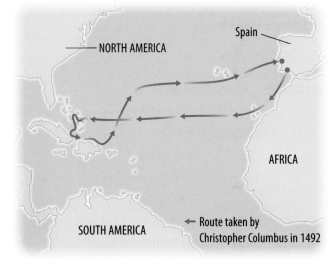

See also: **budget, cost, debt, income, price**

The average American spends more than $2,000 per year on gas. Gas is an **expense**.

explore /ek SPLOR/ (v.)

to travel to a place to learn about it

Spain

NORTH AMERICA

AFRICA

SOUTH AMERICA

← Route taken by Christopher Columbus in 1492

See also: **Columbus, Christopher; conquistador; expedition; Lewis and Clark; Native Americans**

In 1492, the king and queen of Spain sent Christopher Columbus to **explore** new lands.

export /ek SPORT/ (v.)

to send goods to another country to be sold

See also: **goods, import, product, supply and demand**

Countries **export** cars to the United States every year.

61

Ff

factory /FAK tur ee/ (n.)
a place where goods are made by multiple workers

See also: **goods, labor, mass production, product, workforce**

Cars are made in a **factory**.

famine /FAM uhn/ (n.)
a time when most people do not have enough to eat

See also: **agriculture, crop, drought, farming**

There was a **famine** in Ireland in the 1840s. Many people left for the United States to find a better life.

farming /FAHR ming/ (n.)
the raising of crops and animals

See also: **agriculture, cash crop, crop, crop rotation, livestock**

Farming is an important business in the United States. There are more than 2 million farms.

fascism /FASH iz uhm/ (n.)

an idea that the government should have total control and be led by one person or a small group of people

See also: **autocrat; dictator; Hitler, Adolf; Nazi Party; totalitarian**

Adolf Hitler used **fascism** to lead Nazi Germany.

federal government
/FED ur uhl GUHV urn muhnt/ (n.)

the group of people who lead a country and its states or provinces

See also: **branch of government, central government, checks and balances, federalism, government**

The Senate is part of the U.S. **federal government**.

federalism
/FED ur uh liz uhm/ (n.)

a system of government that divides power between the national and state governments

See also: **constitution, federal government, government, state, states' rights**

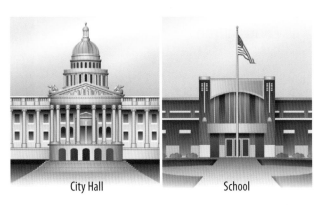

City Hall   School

Federalism allows U.S. states to have their own local governments and to run their own schools.

Federalist /FED ur uh list/ (n.)

a supporter of the
U.S. Constitution
and a strong government

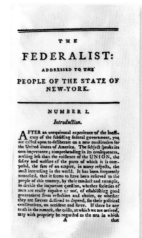

After the American
Revolution, **Federalists**
wrote essays to
explain why people
should support the
Constitution.

See also: **American Revolution;
Anti-Federalist; constitution;
federalism; Hamilton, Alexander**

Federal Reserve System
/FED ur uhl ri ZURV SIS tuhm/ (n.)

a banking system run by the
U.S. government that helps
manage the economy

See also: **bank, commerce,
federal government,
government, money**

One job of the **Federal Reserve System** is to allow
money to be printed.

---

felony /FEL uh nee/ (n.)

a serious crime

See also: **court, due process,
judge, jury, law**

To break into a home and steal is an example
of a **felony**.

Fertile Crescent
/FUR tuhl KRES ent/ (n.)

a part of the Middle East once known for farming

Many ancient civilizations began along the **Fertile Crescent**.

See also: **agriculture; ancient; civilization; Hammurabi, Code of; Middle East**

---

feudalism
/FYOO duhl iz uhm/ (n.)

a way of life in the Middle Ages in which people worked and fought for the nobility in return for land and protection

See also: **agriculture, farming, mercantilism, Middle Ages, peasant**

Lords and their knights owned most of the land in **feudalism**. They rented the land to poor farmers and promised to keep them safe.

Fifteenth Amendment
/FIF teenth uh MEND muhnt/ (n.)

a change to the U.S. Constitution that stated voting rights could not be denied based on race

Most African Americans could not vote until the **Fifteenth Amendment** was passed in 1870.

See also: **amendment, constitution, Nineteenth Amendment, racism, vote**

65

financial institution
/fuh NAN shuhl in stuh TOO shuhn/ (n.)

a business that lends
or invests money

See also: **bank, economy,
investment, money**

A **financial institution**, like a bank, can lend and
borrow money.

First Amendment
/furst uh MEND muhnt/ (n.)

a change to the U.S. Constitution
that lists many of the rights
U.S. citizens have

First Amendment Rights

- *Freedom of Speech*
- *Freedom of Assembly*
- *Freedom of Religion*
- *Freedom of the Press*
- *Freedom to Petition*

See also: **amendment, Bill of Rights,
constitution, freedom, right**

The **First Amendment** is in the Bill of Rights. It
protects important ideas such as freedom of speech.

First Continental Congress
/furst kon tuh NEN tuhl KONG gris/ (n.)

a meeting in 1774 where American
leaders decided that colonies
should set their own laws

See also: **American Revolution, autonomy,
colony, right, self-government**

Representatives from the 13 colonies were at the
First Continental Congress. The Congress wrote
a statement listing the rights of the colonies.

flag /flag/ (n.)
a colored cloth that is a symbol
of a country

See also: **country, nation, state**

The U.S. **flag** has a star for each of its 50 states.

flat boat /flat boht/ (n.)
a long boat used in the past
that carried goods on rivers

See also: **commerce, goods,
Mississippi River, river, trade**

Flat boats were common in the 1800s. Traders used
flat boats to travel on shallow rivers.

foreign policy
/FOR uhn POL uh see/ (n.)
a plan a government
makes for how it acts
toward other nations

See also: **ambassador, diplomat,
government, nation, negotiation**

Part of the United States **foreign policy** is to have
representatives speak to other countries.

67

Fort Sumter /fort SUM tur/ (n.)

a strong building
in South Carolina
that protected soldiers

See also: **civil war; Confederacy;
North, the; soldier; South, the**

In 1861, the Confederate Army attacked **Fort Sumter**.
That attack began the U.S. Civil War.

Founders /FOWN durz/ (n.)

political leaders who helped
create the United States

See also: **American Revolution; constitution;
Franklin, Benjamin; Hamilton, Alexander;
Revolutionary War**

George Washington and Thomas Jefferson were
two **Founders** of the United States.

Fourteenth Amendment
/FOR teenth uh MEND muhnt/ (n.)

a change to the U.S. Constitution
in 1868 that states people born
in the United States are citizens
and are protected by law

See also: **amendment, citizen,
constitution, suffrage**

In the late 1800s, women said that the **Fourteenth
Amendment** gave them the right to vote.

Franklin, Benjamin
/FRANG kluhn, BEN juh muhn/ (n.)
(1706–1790)

an American politician, writer, and scientist

Benjamin Franklin helped draft the Declaration of Independence.

See also: **American Revolution, colony, Declaration of Independence, Founders, politics**

freedom   /FREE duhm/ (n.)

the ability to do and say what you want

See also: **assembly, citizen, civil rights, First Amendment**

All U.S. citizens have the right to **freedom** of speech. They are free to express their opinions in public.

free enterprise
/free EN tur prīz/ (n.)

the right to do business with little government control

See also: **business, commerce, economy, money, trade**

The United States has a lot of **free enterprise**. People may form and run their own businesses.

69

free state /free stayt/ (n.)

a state where slavery
was not allowed

United States in 1860

Ohio

■ Free states

See also: **civil war, slave,
slavery, slave state**

In 1860, Ohio was a **free state**. Owning slaves
was not allowed in Ohio.

French and Indian War
/french end IN dee uhn wor/ (n.)
(1754–1763)

a war between France and
Great Britain for control
of North America

See also: **ally, American Revolution,
colony, Great Britain, Native Americans**

In the **French and Indian War**, both France and
Great Britain had Native American allies.

French Revolution
/french rev uh LOO shuhn/ (n.)
(1787–1799)

an uprising by the people
of France against the monarchy

See also: **civil war, king, monarchy, queen, revolution**

King Louis XVI and Queen Marie Antoinette were killed during the **French Revolution**. They were replaced by a new government.

frontier   /frun TEER/ (n.)

the land at or near the edge
of a settled area

See also: **agrarian; agriculture; farming; migration; West, the**

Farmers and hunters often lived on the **frontier**. Many of them built log houses from trees.

Fugitive Slave Act
/FYOO juh tiv slayv akt/ (n.)

a U.S. law in 1850 that forced
the return of escaped slaves

See also: **free state; North, the; slave; slavery; slave state; South, the**

RUNAWAY SLAVE!

$500 reward
for safe return.

The **Fugitive Slave Act** stated that people in free states had to return escaped slaves to owners in slave states.

71

Gg

generation /jen uh RAY shuhn/ (n.)
people who were born and who grew up during the same time

See also: **ancestor, descendant, era, time period**

A great-grandmother, grandmother, mother, and child are from four different **generations**.

genocide /JEN uh sīd/ (n.)
an attempt to kill all the people of a specific cultural group

See also: **discrimination; ethnicity; Holocaust, the; internment; racism**

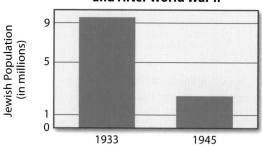

Jewish Population in Europe Before and After World War II

During World War II, nearly 6 million Jewish people were killed in a **genocide**.

geography /jee OG ruh fee/ (n.)
the study of people and places on Earth

See also: **continent, culture, globe, landform, map**

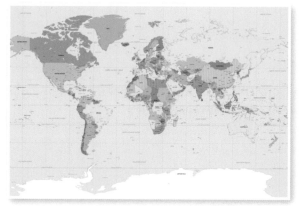

We use maps to learn about the **geography** of the world.

Gettysburg Address
/GET eez burg uh DRES/ (n.)

a speech given by President Abraham Lincoln at Gettysburg, Pennsylvania, in 1863

See also: **battle; civil war; Confederacy; Emancipation Proclamation; Union, the**

The **Gettysburg Address** was a call to unite the country after the U.S. Civil War. The speech became famous around the world.

---

globe /glohb/ (n.)

a world map that shows what the Earth looks like

A **globe** helps you find where different countries and oceans are.

See also: **continent, country, geography, map, ocean**

---

gold /gohld/ (n.)

a valuable yellow metal

Spain became rich when it discovered **gold** in Mexico in the 1500s.

See also: **conquistador, excavate, Gold Rush**

Gold Rush /gohld rush/ (n.)
(1848–1864)

a period when people looked for gold in California

Thousands of people dug for gold during the **Gold Rush**.

See also: **excavate; gold; migration; West, the**

73

goods /gudz/ (n.)

something that people buy
and sell

See also: **allocate, business,
commerce, consumer, trade**

The store sells bread and other **goods**.

government
/GUHV urn muhnt/ (n.)

a group of people that makes
laws and carries them out

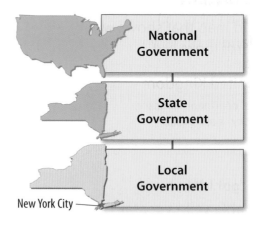

National
Government

State
Government

Local
Government

New York City

See also: **authority, capitol,
law, local, nation**

The U.S. **government** is divided into national, state,
and local **governments**.

governor /GUHV ur nur/ (n.)

the leader of a state

See also: **authority, capitol,
law, politics, state**

A **governor** chooses which bills will become laws
for his or her state.

grand jury   /grand JUR ee/ (n.)

a group of people who decide if a person charged with a crime should go to trial

See also: **court, due process, evidence, jury, law**

The **grand jury** decides if there is enough evidence for a trial.

Great Britain
/grayt BRIT uhn/ (n.)

an island in northwest Europe that is part of the United Kingdom

See also: **American Revolution, country, map, monarchy, nation**

The countries of England, Scotland, and Wales make up **Great Britain**.

Great Depression
/grayt di PRESH uhn/ (n.)
(1929–1939)

a time when many people had little money, little food, and no jobs

See also: **economy, era, money, unemployment**

Many people had to wait in line for food during the **Great Depression**.

75

Great Plains /grayt playnz/ (n.)

the mostly flat middle part
of the United States

Great Plains

See also: **agriculture, location,
Louisiana Purchase, region, state**

The **Great Plains** is a region that includes many
different states in the United States.

gross domestic product (GDP)
/grohs duh MES tik PROD uhkt/ (n.)

the total value of the goods
a country makes in a year

U.S. Gross Domestic Product 2008–2011

See also: **commerce, country,
economy, service**

A country's **gross domestic product** shows how
strong its economy is.

gross income /grohs IN kum/ (n.)

the total amount of money
a person makes

Pay to the order of: Nicole Garcia $1,810.00
****ONE THOUSAND EIGHT HUNDRED TEN AND 0/100 DOLLARS****

First Corner Bank

MEMO June payroll for Nicole Garcia   Signature here

Detach below before depositing

Employee: Nicole Garcia	Gross Income		$2,676.00
Pay period: June 2011	Deductions:		
	Federal Income Tax	$349.00	
	State Income Tax	117.00	
	Social Security	180.00	
	Medicare/Medicare	45.00	
	Insurance	175.00	
	Net Pay		$1,810.00

See also: **earnings, income,
income tax, money, tax**

Gross income is all of the money a person makes
before any taxes are paid.

guild /gild/ (n.)

a group of people in one type of job

See also: **apprentice, commerce, goods, labor union, merchant**

In the past, blacksmiths were part of a **guild**.

gulf /gulf/ (n.)

a part of the sea almost completely surrounded by land

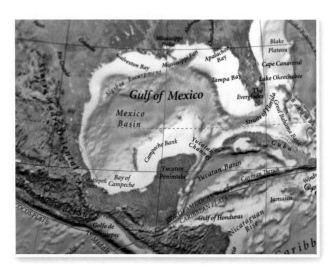

See also: **body of water, ocean, peninsula, physical feature, waterway**

The **Gulf** of Mexico is connected to the Atlantic Ocean.

gunpowder
/GUHN pow dur/ (n.)

a mixture that explodes when burned

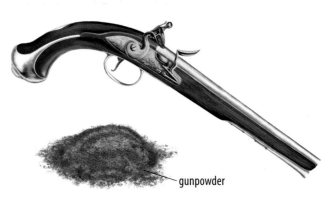

gunpowder

See also: **conflict, defense, frontier, invasion**

The Chinese invented **gunpowder** in the 9th century.

77

Hh

Hamilton, Alexander
/HAM uhl tuhn, al ig ZAN dur/ (n.)
(1757–1804)

a Founder of the United States and the first U.S. Secretary of the Treasury

See also: **American Revolution, Cabinet, constitution, Federalist, Founders**

Alexander Hamilton helped write the *Federalist Papers*. He explained why people should support the U.S. Constitution.

Hammurabi, Code of
/hahm oo RAH bee, kohd uv/ (n.)

one of the earliest sets of written laws, written in 18th century B.C.

See also: **ancient, artifact, city, Fertile Crescent, law**

The people in the ancient city of Babylon lived under the **Code of Hammurabi**.

---

harbor /HAR bur/ (n.)

a body of water where boats find protection from high waves

See also: **body of water, ocean, pilgrim, shelter**

The *Mayflower* sailed into the **harbor** at Plymouth in 1620.

78

Hellenistic /hel uh NIS tik/ (adj.)
(323 B.C.–30 B.C.)

related to Greek history,
culture, or art after the rule
of Alexander the Great

See also: **Ancient Greece, civilization, culture, time period**

The **Hellenistic** period began in 323 B.C.
after the death of Alexander the Great.

Henry, Patrick
/HEN ree, PAT rik/ (n.)
(1736–1799)

an American leader who supported
the American Revolution

In a famous speech,
Patrick Henry told
colonists to fight
the British.

See also: **American Revolution, colony, Great Britain, independence, Revolutionary War**

hieroglyph /HĪ ur uh glif/ (n.)
a picture or symbol used
for language

The Ancient
Egyptians used
hieroglyphs for
writing.

See also: **ancient, civilization, culture, Nile Valley**

79

Hindu-Arabic numerals
/HIN doo AR uh bik NOO mur uhlz/ (n.)

ten digits from an ancient
Indian number system
(0, 1, 2, 3, 4, 5, 6, 7, 8, 9)

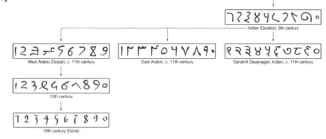

See also: **ancient; civilization; culture;
Hammurabi, Code of**

Most of the world uses **Hindu-Arabic numerals**.

Hinduism /HIN doo iz uhm/ (n.)
a religion common in India

See also: **religion**

Hinduism includes prayer and worship in the home.

history /HIS tur ee/ (n.)
a record of past events

See also: **age, chronology, government,
secondary source**

Reading about **history** can help people understand
modern government and society.

Hitler, Adolf /HIT lur, AY dolf/ (n.)
(1889–1945)

the leader of Germany
from 1933–1945

See also: **dictator, fascism, leader, Nazi Party, war**

Adolf Hitler led Germany into World War II and lost.

Holocaust, the
/HOL uh kawst, THuh/ (n.)

the Nazi killing of Jews during
World War II

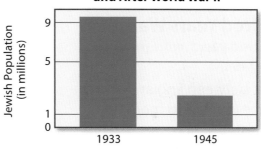

Jewish Population in Europe Before and After World War II

See also: **genocide; Hitler, Adolf; Nazi Party; prejudice; World War II**

Nearly 6 million Jewish people were killed
during **the Holocaust**.

---

homeland /HOHM land/ (n.)
the country in which
a person is born

See also: **country, famine, immigrant, nation, refugee**

Many immigrants left their **homelands** in the 1900s
to start a new life in the United States.

81

House of Representatives
/hows uv rep ri ZEN tuh tivz/ (n.)

  a part of Congress that
  makes laws

See also: **Congress, law, representative, Senate, state**

There are a total of 435 state representatives in the **House of Representatives**.

Hundred Years War
/HUN dred yeerz wor/ (n.)
(1337–1453)

  a war between England and
  France that lasted more than
  a hundred years

The English monarchy fought the French monarchy for control of France in the **Hundred Years War**.

See also: **battle, feudalism, innovation, monarchy**

hunter-gatherer
/HUN tur GATH ur ur/ (n.)

  a member of a group of people
  who moves around and lives
  by hunting, fishing, and
  gathering plants

See also: **age, nomad, subsistence level, time period, tool**

The earliest people lived as **hunter-gatherers**.

Ii

immigrant /IM uh gruhnt/ (n.)

a person who has come
to a new country to live

See also: **country, immigration,
naturalization, population, refugee**

In 2010, 39% of all new **immigrants** came to the
United States from countries in Asia, such as China.

immigration
/im uh GRAY shuhn/ (n.)

the process of people coming
to a new country to live

See also: **country, immigrant,
multicultural, naturalization, refugee**

Ellis Island was a main center for **immigration**
in the United States. **Immigration** through
Ellis Island was highest from 1892 to 1924.

impact /IM pakt/ (n.)

the effect that one thing has
on another

See also: **benefit, consequence,
Great Depression, history**

The **impact** of the Great Depression lasted many years.
People did not have jobs for a long time.

impartial /im PAR shuhl/ (adj.)
treating everyone fairly

The **impartial** judge made a fair decision.

See also: **court, due process, equality, judge, Supreme Court**

impeach /im PEECH/ (v.)
to charge a government official with a crime

See also: **government, House of Representatives, president, trial, vote**

The House of Representatives voted to **impeach** President Andrew Johnson. The trial took place in 1868.

imperialism
/im PEER ee uh liz uhm/ (n.)
one country controlling other countries, especially through force

British Empire in 1915

Canada

India

Australia

■ British territory

See also: **country, empire, expansion, Great Britain, power**

Great Britain created its empire through **imperialism**. The British Empire controlled territory all over the world, including India, Canada, and Australia.

import /im PORT/ (v.)

to bring products from one
country into another country

See also: **country, export,
goods, product, trade**

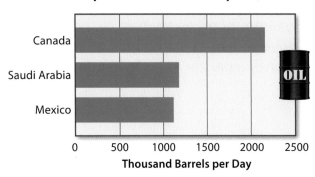

Top Sources of U.S. Oil Imports, 2011

The United States **imports** most of its oil from Canada.

Inca /ING kuh/ (n.)

a group of native people who
had a large civilization in Peru

See also: **Aztec, civilization,
culture, empire, Maya**

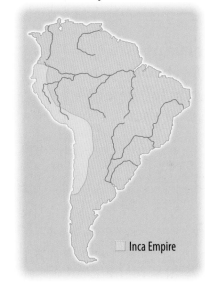

Inca Empire in 1532

☐ Inca Empire

The **Inca** ruled
in the 1400s
and early 1500s.
Their empire
included large
parts of South
America.

---

income /IN kum/ (n.)

money earned

See also: **earnings, income tax,
money, per capita income, profit**

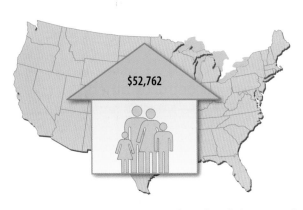

$52,762

In 2010, the median **income** for a family living in the
United States was $52,762 per year.

income tax /IN kum taks/ (n.)

an amount of money paid to the government based on how much money a person or business earns

See also: **earnings, income, money, sales tax, tax**

Americans paid over a trillion dollars in **income taxes** on their earnings in 2011.

indentured servant
/in DEN churd SUR vuhnt/ (n.)

a person who works for someone without payment for a set amount of time

See also: **colony, freedom, immigrant, labor, slave**

Some new settlers came to the American colonies as **indentured servants**. They worked to pay for their trip.

independence
/in di PEN duhns/ (n.)

freedom from control by others

See also: **American Revolution, autonomy, colony, freedom, liberty**

The colonies fought for **independence** from Great Britain.

Indian Removal Act

/IN dee uhn ri MOO vuhl akt/ (n.)

a law signed by President Andrew Jackson in 1830 that forced Native Americans to leave their land

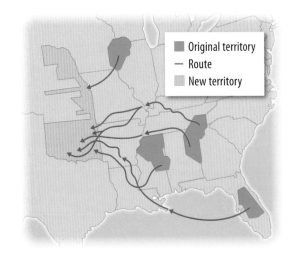

Original territory
— Route
New territory

See also: **law, Native Americans, president, reservation**

Native Americans had to leave their homes because of the **Indian Removal Act**. They were forced to move west.

Indian Territory

/IN dee uhn TER uh tor ee/ (n.)

the land where Native Americans were forced to move to in 1830 under the Indian Removal Act

Indian Territory, 1830

See also: **law, Native Americans, president, reservation, Trail of Tears**

The **Indian Territory** included what is now known as Oklahoma and part of Nebraska and Kansas.

individual right

/in duh VIJ oo uhl rīt/ (n.)

a right that the law says each citizen should have

The right to free speech is an **individual right** of U.S. citizens.

See also: **Bill of Rights, citizen, Declaration of Independence, freedom, law**

87

industrialization
/in DUS tree uhl i ZAY shuhn/ (n.)

the growth of factories
instead of farms
in an area

See also: **business, civil war, factory, Industrial Revolution, industry**

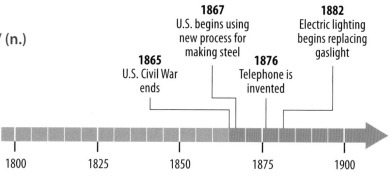

1865
U.S. Civil War
ends

1867
U.S. begins using
new process for
making steel

1876
Telephone is
invented

1882
Electric lighting
begins replacing
gaslight

1800   1825   1850   1875   1900

Industrialization grew in the United States
after the U.S. Civil War.

Industrial Revolution
/in DUS tree uhl
rev uh LOO shuhn/ (n.)
(1760–1850)

a time when new machines and
inventions changed how people
lived and worked

See also: **Great Britain, industrialization, industry, innovation, mass production**

The **Industrial Revolution** began in Great Britain.
Many people moved from farms in the country
to work in factories in the cities.

---

industry /IN duh stree/ (n.)

the people and businesses
involved in making
a certain product

See also: **business, industrialization, Industrial Revolution, mass production, product**

The technology **industry** has been growing in the
United States since the 1860s.

inflation /in FLAY shuhn/ (n.)

an increase in available money
that causes prices to go up

See also: **cost, deflation, money, price, scarcity**

Not having enough of a product can cause an
inflation in prices.

infrastructure
/IN fruh struk chur/ (n.)

the basic systems and services
needed to run properly

See also: **business, city, country, region, transportation**

The **infrastructure** of a city includes roads, bridges,
and electricity.

inhabitant
/in HAB uh tuhnt/ (n.)

a person who lives in a
certain place

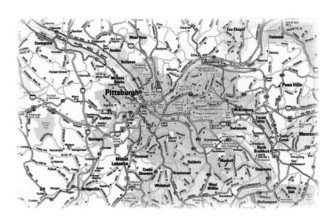

See also: **city, civilization, population**

In 2010, the city of Pittsburgh had over 300,000
inhabitants.

innovation
/in uh VAY shuhn/ (n.)

a new idea, product, or process

The assembly line was an important **innovation** in 1913. It was a faster way to build cars.

See also: **assembly line, Industrial Revolution, invention, mass production, transportation**

---

inset map   /IN set map/ (n.)

a part of a map that makes a certain area of the map bigger

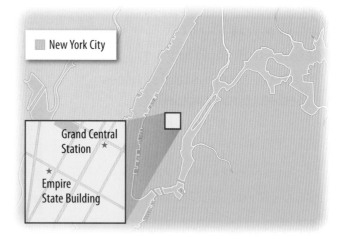

City maps often have **inset maps** to show the specific locations of tourist attractions.

See also: **compass rose, map, map key, map scale**

---

institution
/in stuh TOO shuhn/ (n.)

a large organization that does a certain type of work

A hospital is an example of an **institution**. People receive health services at hospitals.

See also: **bank, business, financial institution, service**

integration
/in tuh GRAY shuhn/ (n.)

the act of bringing people of different abilities, races, or religions together

See also: ***Brown v. Board of Education***, **equality**, ***Plessy v. Ferguson***, **racism**, **segregation**

Brown v. Board of Education was a famous court case. It ordered the racial **integration** of schools in 1954.

interdependence
/in tur di PEN duhns/ (n.)

a state in which two or more countries or people need each other

See also: **economy**, **equality**, **goods**, **independence**

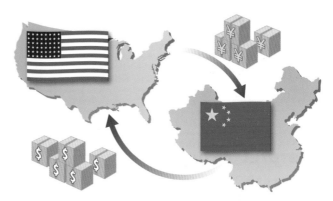

The United States and China have economic **interdependence**. The two countries buy the goods they need from one another.

interest /IN tur ist/ (n.)

the amount of money a person pays for borrowing money

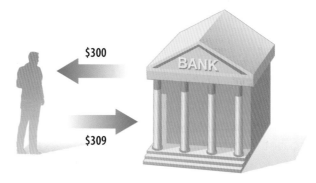

$300

BANK

$309

Interest: $300.00 x 3% = $9.00

See also: **bank**, **currency**, **debt**, **loan**, **money**

The man borrowed $300 from the bank with 3% **interest**. He paid back $309. The $9 was the amount he owed the bank in **interest**.

91

intermediate direction
/in tur MEE dee it duh REK shuhn/ (n.)

a direction between the cardinal directions north, south, east, and west

See also: **cardinal direction, compass, compass rose, location, map**

The **intermediate directions** include northwest (NW) and southwest (SW). They also include northeast (NE) and southeast (SE).

---

internment /in TURN muhnt/ (n.)

the act of keeping a large group of people in one place during a war

The U.S. government forced the **internment** of 100,000 Japanese Americans during World War II.

See also: **Hitler, Adolf; Holocaust, the; politics; prejudice; World War II**

---

interpret /in TUR prit/ (v.)

to explain the meaning of something

See also: **constitution, justice, law, Supreme Court, unconstitutional**

The role of the Supreme Court justices is to **interpret** the U.S. Constitution.

---

interview /IN tur vyoo/ (n.)

a meeting where a person asks another person questions to get information

See also: **communication, negotiation, occupation, testimony**

At a job **interview**, a person answers questions about his or her education and past work.

invasion /in VAY zhuhn/ (n.)

the act of entering a place
by force to try to control it

See also: **Nazi Party, Vietnam War,
War of 1812, World War I, World War II**

The Nazi **invasion** of Poland happened in 1939.
This event started World War II.

invention /in VEN shuhn/ (n.)

a new product that
someone makes

Alexander Graham Bell
invented the telephone
in 1876. This **invention**
gave people a new way
to communicate.

See also: **Bell, Alexander Graham;
communication; Industrial Revolution;
innovation; product**

investment /in VEST muhnt/ (n.)

a purchase that may make
more money in the future

See also: **earnings, money, profit,
stock, stockholder**

Stocks can be a good **investment**. A stockholder can
sell his or her stock later when it is worth more money.

Iron Curtain
/ī urn KURT uhn/ (n.)

a made-up line between eastern and western countries in Europe

See also: **border; Cold War, the; communism; conflict; World War II**

The **Iron Curtain** was created after World War II. It separated communist countries from democratic countries.

---

irrigation /ir uh GAY shuhn/ (n.)

the system of supplying water to people, plants, or animals

See also: **agriculture, aqueduct, crop, farming**

Farmers use a system of **irrigation** to water their crops when the weather is dry and there is little rain.

Islam /i SLAHM/ (n.)

the beliefs and practices of people who follow the teachings of Muhammad

See also: **Middle East, monotheism, mosque, Muslim, religion**

People who practice **Islam** are called Muslims. The symbol of **Islam** is shown on some flags.

isolationism

/ī suh LAY shuhn iz uhm/ (n.)

the idea of being separate from others

See also: **country, impact, neutral, World War I, World War II**

Some Americans supported **isolationism** during World War II. They did not want the U.S. to get involved in the fight between other countries.

issue /ISH oo/ (n.)

an important topic

THE NEWS

VOL.24   ISSUE 18   Daily news   Wednesday, February 12th

UNEMPLOYMENT AT AN ALL-TIME HIGH

See also: **candidate, conflict, debate, election, unemployment**

Newspapers will write about important **issues**. People sometimes have different opinions on these **issues**.

isthmus /IS muhs/ (n.)

a thin area of land with water on each side that joins two larger areas of land

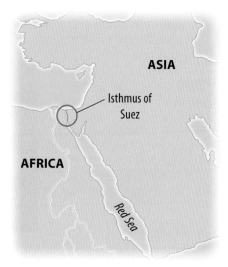

ASIA

Isthmus of Suez

AFRICA

Red Sea

The **Isthmus** of Suez connects Africa and Asia.

See also: **cape, country, geography, landform, peninsula**

Jj

Jim Crow laws
/jim kroh lawz/ (n.)
(1877–1954)

the unfair rules in the South that kept African Americans separate from whites

See also: **civil rights, discrimination, *Plessy v. Ferguson*, racism, segregation**

Jim Crow laws kept African Americans from using the same water fountains as whites.

Judaism /JOO dee iz uhm/ (n.)

the main religion practiced by Jewish people

See also: **monotheism, religion, synagogue**

The symbol of **Judaism** is the Star of David. It is a star with six points.

judge /juj/ (n.)

a person in charge of making decisions in court

See also: **evidence, impartial, justice, law, legal**

A **judge** listens to all proof presented in a case.

jury /JUR ee/ (n.)

a group of people who listen to a trial and decide the outcome

See also: **court, grand jury, judge, law, legal**

People on a **jury** must decide if someone on trial is guilty or not guilty.

justice /JUS tis/ (n.)

1. the act of being fair

See also: **civil rights, equality, Jim Crow laws, segregation**

People protested the Jim Crow laws to demand **justice** for African Americans.

2. a judge in the Supreme Court

See also: **constitution, impartial, interpret, law, Supreme Court**

The Supreme Court **justices** are responsible for interpreting the U.S. Constitution.

Kk

king   /king/ (n.)
the male ruler of a monarchy

See also: **authority, leader, monarchy, power, queen**

King George I was the **king** of Great Britain from 1714 to 1727. **King** Abdullah II has been the **king** of Jordan since 1999.

King, Jr., Dr. Martin Luther
/king, joon yur, DOK tur MART uhn LOO thur/ (n.)
(1929–1968)

an African American leader of the U.S. Civil Rights movement

See also: **civil rights; civil war; equality; freedom; Parks, Rosa**

Dr. Martin Luther King, Jr. led marches to demand that African Americans have the same rights as whites.

Korean Conflict
/koh REE uhn KON flikt/ (n.)
(1945–1950)

a war between North Korea and South Korea

North Korea

South Korea

During the **Korean Conflict**, the United States helped South Korea, and China helped North Korea.

See also: **communism, conflict, demarcation line, Vietnam War**

labor /LAY bur/ (n.)

a group of workers

See also: **agriculture, economy, factory, labor union, workforce**

Farms and factories need **labor**.

labor union

/LAY bur YOO nyuhn/ (n.)

a group of workers who unite to protect their rights

See also: **guild, labor, negotiation, right, workforce**

A **labor union** can ask a company to pay its workers more money.

Lafayette, Marquis de

/lah fee ET, mahr KEE duh/ (n.)
(1757–1834)

a French military leader who fought with the colonists in the American Revolution

Marquis de Lafayette fought for George Washington and the American army in the Revolutionary War.

See also: **American Revolution, colony, military, politics, Revolutionary War**

99

landform /LAND form/ (n.)
a natural feature on Earth

See also: **geography, landmark, mountain, physical feature, Rocky Mountains**

The Rocky Mountains are a major **landform** in North America.

landmark /LAND mark/ (n.)
an important location

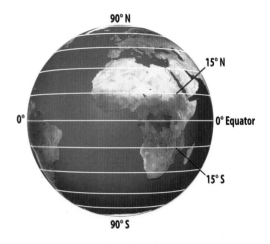

See also: **geography, landform, mountain, physical feature, Statue of Liberty**

A **landmark** can be natural or man-made.

latitude line /LAT uh tood līn/ (n.)
an imaginary line that runs east to west around the globe (also known as a parallel)

See also: **geography, globe, longitude line, map, parallel**

A **latitude line** shows the distance in degrees north or south of the equator.

law /law/ (n.)

a rule that all people in a certain place must follow

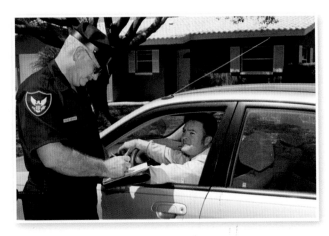

See also: **court, defendant, judge, justice, legal**

Police officers make sure that people follow the **law**.

leader /LEE dur/ (n.)

a person with power who directs a group of people

See also: **authority, bill, law, power, president**

The **leader** of the United States is the president.

legal /LEE guhl/ (adj.)

allowed by law

See also: **bill, Congress, justice, law, legislation**

The **legal** age to drive in most U.S. states is 16.

legislation /le jis LAY shun/ (n.)

a law or group of laws

See also: **civil rights, Jim Crow laws, law, prejudice**

The Jim Crow laws are an example of unfair **legislation**.

Lewis and Clark
/LOO is end klark/ (n.)
(Meriwether Lewis, 1774–1809)
(William Clark, 1770–1838)

two Americans who explored the Louisiana Purchase and the land around it from 1804 to 1806

See also: **expansion, expedition, explore, Louisiana Purchase, Manifest Destiny**

President Thomas Jefferson sent **Lewis and Clark** to learn what was in the new U.S. land. They took notes on the plants, animals, and people.

libel   /LĪ buhl/ (n.)

the act of writing information
about someone that is not true

See also: **bias, court, legal, media**

The Daily Sun was found guilty of **libel**. It printed
a false story about the mayor.

---

liberty   /LIB ur tee/ (n.)

the state of being free
from control

See also: **American Revolution,
constitution, freedom, Great Britain,
independence**

The **Liberty** Bell stands for America's independence
from Great Britain. After the American Revolution,
Americans gained their **liberty**.

---

limited government
/LIM uh tid GUHV urn muhnt/ (n.)

the idea that all citizens,
including government leaders,
must obey the law

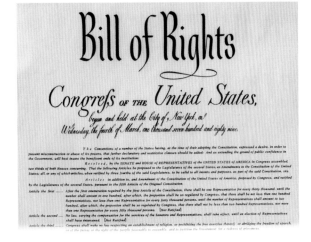

See also: **autonomy, Bill of Rights,
constitution, principle,
unlimited government**

The United States has a **limited government**.
Everybody has to obey the laws in the U.S.
Constitution.

limited resource
/LIM uh tid REE sors/ (n.)

   a part of nature that people can use but cannot replace

See also: **natural resource, non-renewable resource, ore, renewable resource, resource**

Coal is a **limited resource**. People use coal more quickly than it can be replaced.

livestock /LĪV stok/ (n.)
   animals raised on a farm

See also: **agrarian, agriculture, farming**

Livestock includes horses, cows, and sheep.

loan /lohn/ (v.)
   to give money that must be returned

See also: **bank, business, commerce, entrepreneur, financial institution**

Banks **loan** money to people to help them start their own businesses.

local /LOH kuhl/ (adj.)
related to the nearby area

Federal Government	
State Government	
Local Government	

See also: **city, county, government, law, power**

Counties in U.S. states have their own **local** governments. **Local** governments have duties that include building roads and making sure people follow the law.

location /loh KAY shuhn/ (n.)
a position or place

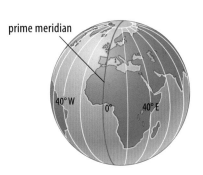

See also: **absolute location, cardinal direction, compass rose, latitude line, longitude line**

The **location** of the fire station is on the corner of Main Street and First Avenue.

longitude line
/LON juh tood līn/ (n.)

an imaginary line that runs from the North Pole to the South Pole (also known as a meridian)

prime meridian

40° W   0°   40° E

See also: **geography, latitude line, map, parallel, prime meridian**

A **longitude line** shows the distance in degrees east or west of the prime meridian.

105

Louisiana Purchase
/loo ee zee AN uh PUR chuhs/ (n.)

the sale of the Louisiana Territory from France to the United States in 1803

See also: **expansion; frontier; Manifest Destiny; West, the**

The **Louisiana Purchase** doubled the size of the United States. The U.S. government paid France $15 million dollars for the land.

Loyalist /LOI uh list/ (n.)

an American colonist who supported Great Britain during the Revolutionary War

See also: **allegiance, American Revolution, Great Britain, independence**

Many thousands of **Loyalists** went to live in Canada after the American Revolution.

majority /muh JOR uh tee/ (n.)

more than half of the number of people or items in a group

School Elections

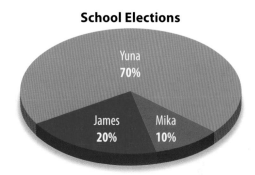

See also: **candidate, democracy, election, Electoral College, vote**

Yuna won 70% of the votes for her school election. She won the **majority** of the votes.

Manifest Destiny
/MAN uh fest DES tuh nee/ (n.)

the belief during the 1800s that America should own all land on the North American continent

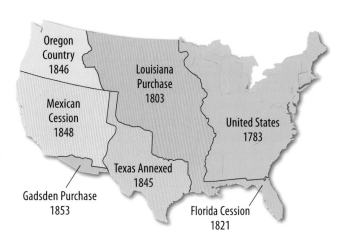

See also: **coast; expansion; pioneer; settler; West, the**

The belief in **Manifest Destiny** led the United States to expand its territory from the Atlantic coast all the way to the Pacific coast.

manufacturing
/man yuh FAK chur ing/ (n.)

the process of making things
for people to buy

See also: **business, factory,
industrialization, industry,
product**

The **manufacturing** of cars is an important industry
in the United States. More than 2.7 million cars were
manufactured in the United States in 2010.

map /map/ (n.)

a drawing that shows all
or part of a place

See also: **compass rose,
latitude line, longitude line,
map key, map scale**

The **map** of the United States shows the boundaries
of all 50 states.

map key /map KEE/ (n.)

a list (usually in a box) that explains how to understand symbols or colors on a map

See also: **geography, landmark, map, physical feature**

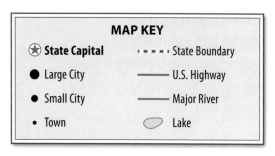

The **map key** shows that a star with a circle around it is the symbol for a state capital.

map scale /map skayl/ (n.)

a ruled line that shows how distances on a map are related to real distances

See also: **location, map, map key**

The **map scale** shows that the Lincoln Memorial and the Washington Monument are one mile apart.

market economy
/MAR kit i KON uh mee/ (n.)

an economic system in which citizens, not governments, own and run companies

See also: **business, capitalism, economy, government, price**

Companies decide which goods to sell in a **market economy**. Companies also decide what the prices of these goods will be.

Mason-Dixon Line
/MAY suhn DIK suhn līn/ (n.)

the dividing line between slave states and free states before the U.S. Civil War

See also: **civil war; free state; North, the; slave state; South, the**

Pennsylvania

The Mason-Dixon Line

Maryland

Delaware

Virginia

The **Mason-Dixon Line** helped form the borders of Pennsylvania, Maryland, and Delaware.

mass production
/mas pruh DUK shuhn/ (n.)

the act of making a large number of products

See also: **assembly line, cost, factory, goods, industrialization**

The **mass production** of cars on an assembly line began in 1913 in Michigan.

Maya /MĪ uh/ (n.)

a group of native people who had a large civilization in Mexico and Central America

See also: **Aztec, civilization, empire, Native Americans**

The **Maya** were very powerful from A.D. 250 to A.D. 900. Some of the temples they built during this time still stand today.

Mayflower Compact
/MAY flow ur KOM pakt/ (n.)

a plan of government prepared
by the Pilgrims who sailed
on the *Mayflower*

See also: **colony, government,
law, pilgrim**

All of the male Pilgrims signed the **Mayflower
Compact** on November 21, 1620. They agreed
to follow the laws of the new colony.

---

mayor   /MAY ur/ (n.)

an elected leader of a city
or town

See also: **city, community,
government, leader, vote**

In some U.S. cities, the **mayor** has the power
to select the police chief and other officials.

---

media   /MEE dee uh/ (n.)

the different ways to send
information to people

See also: **communication, current,
distribution, printing press, society**

Smartphones, tablets, newspapers, magazines, and
television are all different types of **media**.

111

Mediterranean
/med uh tuh RAY nee uhn/ (adj.)

related to the Mediterranean Sea or the lands or people around it

See also: **coast, merchant, Middle East, region, trade**

The **Mediterranean** region is made up of the coastal lands that surround the **Mediterranean** Sea. It includes countries in Europe, Asia, and Africa.

mercantilism
/MUR kuhn ti liz uhm/ (n.)

an idea in which countries sold more goods to other countries than they bought from them

See also: **business, century, colony, economy, gold**

Mercantilism helped make many European countries stronger. They sold many goods to their colonies and made a lot of money.

merchant /MUR chuhnt/ (n.)

a person who buys and sells products to make money

See also: **business, cost, goods, money, price**

A flower **merchant** buys flowers at one price. The merchant then sells them to customers at a higher price.

meridian /muh RID ee uhn/ (n.)

an imaginary line that runs from the North Pole to the South Pole (also known as a longitude line)

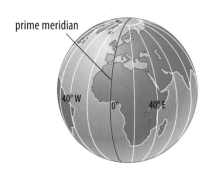

prime meridian

40° W   0°   40° E

See also: **globe, latitude line, longitude line, parallel, prime meridian**

The zero degree line of longitude is called the prime **meridian**.

mesa /MAY suh/ (n.)

a steep hill with a flat top

See also: **landform; mountain; mountain range; plateau; Southwest, the**

A **mesa** is a landform that looks like a table. It is made of hard rock.

metropolitan area
/met ruh POL uh tuhn AIR ee uh/ (n.)

a large city and the area around it

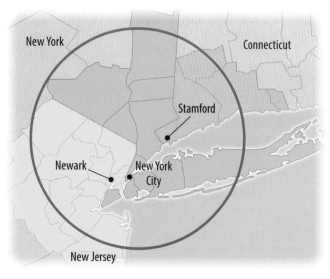

New York   Connecticut

Stamford

Newark   New York City

New Jersey

See also: **city, nation, population, suburb, urban**

The **metropolitan area** of New York City includes large cities in New Jersey and Connecticut.

113

Mexican-American War

/MEK suh kuhn uh MER uh kuhn wor/ (n.)

(1846–1848)

a war between Mexico and the United States

See also: **battle; expansion; Manifest Destiny; Southwest, the**

The United States defeated Mexico in the **Mexican-American War** and gained Mexican territory.

Middle Ages

/MID uhl AY jiz/ (n.)

a time in Europe from about A.D. 500 to A.D. 1500

See also: **age, Christianity, church, history, time period**

Many large churches, called cathedrals, were built during the **Middle Ages**.

Middle East /MID uhl eest/ (n.)

an area near the Mediterranean Sea that includes countries in Europe, Asia, and Africa

See also: **country, Fertile Crescent, Mediterranean, Ottoman Empire**

Egypt is a country in the **Middle East**.

migrant worker
/MĪ gruhnt WUR kur/ (n.)

a person who moves from place
to place to find work

See also: **immigrant, labor, migration, region, workforce**

There are over 3 million **migrant workers** in the
United States. A **migrant worker** usually works
on a farm.

---

migration   /mī GRAY shuhn/ (n.)

the movement of people
from one place to another

See also: **immigrant; immigration; migrant worker; region; South, the**

During the Great **Migration** of 1916-1970, about
6 million African Americans moved from the South
to the North to work in factories.

---

military
/MIL uh ter ee/ (n.)

the soldiers of a country

See also: **battle, country, defense, national security, soldier**

A **military** protects its country.

115

millennium (millennia)
/muh LEN ee uhm
(muh LEN ee uh)/ (n.)

a period of 1,000 years

See also: **century, decade, era, time period**

On January 1st, 2000, people around the world celebrated the start of the new **millennium**.

mission /MISH uhn/ (n.)
a place where people do religious work

Colonists from Spain built many **missions** in the Southwest to teach Native Americans about Christianity.

See also: **Christianity, church, colony, Native Americans, religion**

Mississippi River
/mis uh SIP ee RIV ur/ (n.)

the longest river in North America

The **Mississippi River** flows from Minnesota to the Gulf of Mexico.

monarchy /MON ur kee/ (n.)

a government with a king
and/or queen

Queen Elizabeth II
is the head of the
British **monarchy**.

See also: **government, king,
leader, power, queen**

money /MUN ee/ (n.)

something of value used to pay
for goods and services

See also: **currency, goods,
service, wealth**

Paper **money** was invented in China
over 1,000 years ago.

monopoly /muh NOP uh lee/ (n.)

a company that has complete
control over an industry

See also: **business, goods,
industry, product, service**

John D. Rockefeller had a **monopoly** on the U.S.
oil industry from the 1880s to 1911. His company
controlled 90% of the oil production.

monotheism
/MAH nuh thee i zuhm/ (n.)

the belief that there is
only one god

See also: **Christianity, Islam,
Judaism, religion**

Followers of Islam, Christianity, and Judaism all
practice **monotheism**.

mosque /mosk/ (n.)

a place where Muslims worship

See also: **Islam, Middle East,
monotheism, Muslim, religion**

The oldest **mosque** in the world is in Saudi Arabia.
It was built in A.D. 622.

Mound Builders
/MOWND BIL durz/ (n.)

a group of Native Americans
who built different types
of hills between about
A.D. 900 and A.D. 1200

See also: **ancient, archaeologist,
culture, Native Americans**

Mound Builders built the Great Serpent
Mound around A.D. 1000. The mounds are
made of earth, shells, and other objects.

mountain /MOWN tuhn/ (n.)

a high area of land
with steep sides

See also: **altitude, landform,
mountain range, physical feature,
Rocky Mountains**

Mount Everest is the tallest **mountain** in the world.

mountain range
/MOWN tuhn raynj/ (n.)

a group of mountains that are
connected or next to each other

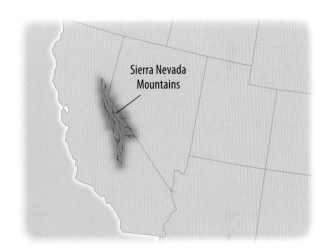

Sierra Nevada
Mountains

See also: **altitude, geography, landform,
mountain, Rocky Mountains**

The Sierra Nevada is a **mountain range** in California.
It is more than 250 miles long.

movement /MOOV muhnt/ (n.)

a number of actions a group takes
to achieve a shared goal

See also: **civic participation, civil rights,
equality, passive resistance,
women's suffrage movement**

The civil rights **movement** began in the 1950s.
It called for equal rights for African Americans.

multicultural
/mul ti KUL chur uhl/ (adj.)

of many different cultures

Classrooms in the United States are some of the most **multicultural** classrooms in the world.

See also: **culture, custom, diversity, ethnicity, immigrant**

Muslim /MUZ luhm/ (n.)

a person who believes in and practices Islam

Prayer is an important part of being a **Muslim**.

See also: **Islam, Middle East, monotheism, mosque, religion**

nation /NAY shuhn/ (n.)

a country that has its own government

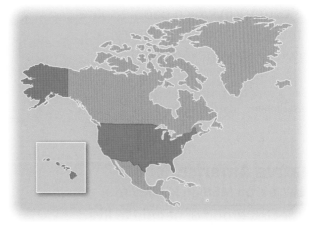

See also: **city-state, country, government, nation-state, state**

The United States is the fourth largest **nation** in the world.

---

nationalism

/NASH uh nuh li zuhm/ (n.)

strong loyalty and pride for one's country

See also: **allegiance, country, liberty, patriot, Revolutionary War**

After the Revolutionary War, Americans had a lot of **nationalism**. They were proud to be part of a free country.

---

national security

/NASH uh nuhl si KYUR uh tee/ (n.)

the safety of a country's people and information

See also: **citizen, country, government, military, terrorism**

Government groups protect the **national security** of the United States.

nation-state
/NAY shuhn stayt/ (n.)

a country in which people share the same language, history, culture, and government

See also: **city-state, country, government, nation, state**

Japan is a **nation-state** because its people share the same culture and government.

JAPAN

Native Americans
/NAY tiv uh MER uh kuhnz/ (n.)

the first group of people to live in North America

Northwest Coast

Plateau

Great Basin

Great Plains

Woodland

Southwest

California

Southeast

See also: **French and Indian War, Indian Removal Act, Indian Territory, oral history, Trail of Tears**

Before the first European settlers arrived in 1585, **Native Americans** lived in different regions all over the United States.

---

naturalization
/NACH ur uh li ZAY shuhn/ (n.)

the way for a person who is born in one country to become a citizen of another country

See also: **allegiance, citizen, country, immigrant, immigration**

People who apply for **naturalization** in the United States must take the Oath of Allegiance before they can become a citizen.

natural resource
/NACH ur uhl REE sors/ (n.)

a part of nature that people can use

See also: **limited resource, non-renewable resource, renewable resource, resource**

Soil is a **natural resource** that people use to grow food.

Nazi Party
/NAHT see PAR tee/ (n.)

a group that ruled Germany from 1933 to 1945

See also: **fascism; Hitler, Adolf; Holocaust, the; nationalism; World War II**

Adolf Hitler started the **Nazi Party** in Germany in 1920.

need /need/ (n.)
something that a person must have in order to live

See also: **budget, consumer, supply and demand, want**

Food, clothing, and shelter are all **needs**.

negotiation
/ni goh shee AY shuhn/ (n.)

a discussion between people
or groups who want to come
to an agreement

See also: **agreement, communication,
compromise, conflict, diplomat**

Former U.S. President Bill Clinton led peace **negotiations**
between the leaders of Israel and Palestine in 1993.

neutral /NOO truhl/ (adj.)

not taking sides in an argument
or war

See also: **Allied Powers, Central Powers,
isolationism, World War II**

The United States had hoped to remain **neutral**
in World War II.

Nile Valley /nīl VAL ee/ (n.)

the region along the
Nile River where Egyptian
civilization began

See also: **ancient, civilization, crop,
culture, Fertile Crescent**

The land in the **Nile Valley** was good for growing crops.

Nineteenth Amendment
/nīn TEENTH uh MEND muhnt / (n.)

a change made to the
U.S. Constitution in 1920
that gave women the right
to vote

See also: **amendment, constitution, ratify, suffrage, vote**

The women's movement for voting rights began
in 1848. The **Nineteenth Amendment** was added
to the U.S. Constitution more than 70 years later.

---

nomad /NOH mad/ (n.)

a person who moves from place
to place

See also: **culture, hunter-gatherer, tradition**

Nomads move from one place to another to find
food. Long ago, many people were **nomads**.

---

nominate /NOM uh nayt/ (v.)

to suggest a person for a position

See also: **election, Electoral College, Senate, Supreme Court, vote**

The president **nominates** justices to the Supreme
Court. The U.S. Senate then decides whether
to approve the nomination.

125

non-renewable resource
/non ri NOO uh buhl REE sors/ (n.)

a part of nature that people can use but cannot replace

Crude oil is a **non-renewable resource** because it takes millions of years to form. People use oil faster than the Earth makes it.

See also: **limited resource, natural resource, ore, renewable resource, resource**

non-violence
/non VĪ uh luhns/ (n.)

the practice of peaceful actions to reach a goal

Civil rights protesters believed in **non-violence**. They had peaceful marches and sit-ins.

See also: **civic participation; civil rights; King, Jr., Dr. Martin Luther; passive resistance**

norm   /norm/ (n.)

a way that most people act

In the United States, it is the **norm** to shake hands when you first meet someone.

See also: **common, culture, custom, society, tradition**

North, the /north, тниuh/ (n.)

the group of northern states that stayed in the Union during the U.S. Civil War

Union States

See also: **civil war; region; secede; South, the; Union, the**

The army for **the North** was called the Union Army.

Northwest Ordinance of 1787

/north **WEST ORD** uhn uhns uv sev uhn **TEEN AY** tee **SEV** uhn/ (n.)

an act passed by Congress that stated the Northwest Territory had to be divided into smaller territories

Northwest Territory, 1787

Minnesota

Wisconsin

Michigan

Mississippi River

Illinois Indiana Ohio

Ohio River

See also: **Congress, frontier, law, ordinance, territory**

The Northwest Territory would later be divided into six new states because of the **Northwest Ordinance of 1787**.

127

Oo

occupation
/ok yuh PAY shuhn/ (n.)

a job

See also: **factory, labor, labor union, specialize, workforce**

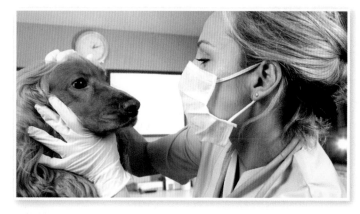

The job of veterinarian is one of the fastest-growing **occupations** in the United States.

ocean /OH shuhn/ (n.)

a large body of salt water

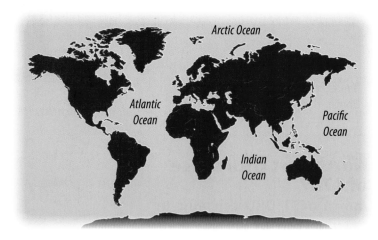

See also: **body of water, canal, landform, pollution, river**

There are four main **oceans** on Earth: Atlantic, Pacific, Indian, and Arctic.

oligarchy
/AH luh gar kee/ (n.)

a government that is controlled by a small number of people

The city-state of Athens was controlled by an **oligarchy** after it lost the Peloponnesian War to Sparta.

See also: **Athens, city-state, democracy, monarchy, Peloponnesian War**

OPEC /OH pek/ (n.)

(Organization of the Petroleum Exporting Countries) a group of countries that sells petroleum to other countries

See also: **petroleum, scarcity, subsidy, supply and demand**

OPEC decides how much oil to send to other countries and how much to charge for it.

---

oral history
/OR uhl HIS tur ee/ (n.)

a spoken record and story passed from one generation to the next

See also: **culture, custom, generation, Native Americans, tradition**

Native Americans practiced **oral history**.

---

ordinance /ORD uhn uhns/ (n.)

an official order from the government

See also: **government, law, legislation, Northwest Ordinance of 1787, rule**

The United States passed an **ordinance** in 1787. It stated that the Northwest Territory would have to be divided into smaller territories.

129

ore /or/ (n.)

a rock that contains metal
and other minerals

See also: **limited resource,
natural resource,
non-renewable resource,
resource**

Iron and steel are made from **ore**.

Ottoman Empire
/OT uh muhn EM pīr/ (n.)
(1300–1922)

a group of countries in Europe,
North Africa, and the Middle East
that were controlled by people
from Turkey

EUROPE

Black Sea

Mediterranean Sea

ASIA

AFRICA

Medina

Mecca

■ The Ottoman Empire,
1683–1699

Red Sea

See also: **empire, Islam,
Middle East, power**

In the 1500s, the **Ottoman Empire** took control
of Mecca and Medina, the two most important
cities of Islam.

130

Pp

Paine, Thomas
/payn, TOM uhs/ (n.)
(1737–1809)

a writer who supported the American Revolution

See also: **American Revolution, Declaration of Independence, Founders, Great Britain, patriot**

Thomas Paine wrote *Common Sense* in 1776. He said the American colonies should be free from Great Britain.

Panama Canal
/PAN uh mah kuh NAL/ (n.)

a waterway built between the Atlantic and Pacific Oceans

See also: **canal, ocean, trade, transportation, waterway**

The **Panama Canal** makes travel by ship much faster because it connects two oceans.

parallel /PA ruh lel/ (n.)

an imaginary line that runs from east to west around the Earth

See also: **absolute location, globe, latitude line, longitude line, meridian**

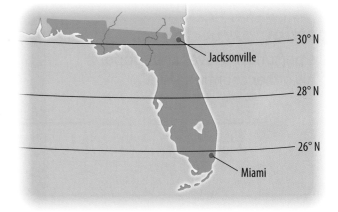

Miami is near the 26th **parallel**. Jacksonville is near the 30th **parallel**.

131

Parks, Rosa
/parks, ROH zuh/ (n.)
(1913–2005)

a civil rights leader

See also: **civil rights, equality, passive resistance, racism, segregation**

On December 1, 1955, **Rosa Parks** would not give her bus seat to a white person. This act helped start the U.S. civil rights movement.

passive resistance
/PAS iv ri ZIS tuhns/ (n.)

a peaceful way to disagree

See also: **civil rights; equality; King, Jr., Dr. Martin Luther; movement; non-violence**

African Americans practiced **passive resistance** during the Montgomery Bus Boycott of 1955-1956. They walked to work instead of taking the bus.

patriot   /PAY tree uht/ (n.)

a person who loves and supports his or her country

See also: **allegiance, country, nationalism, Pledge of Allegiance, soldier**

A soldier will fight to keep his or her country safe. A soldier is a **patriot**.

peasant   /PEZ ent/ (n.)

a poor farmer or farm worker who works on a small piece of land

See also: **agrarian, farming, feudalism, labor, poverty**

In Europe long ago, **peasants** grew food on farms owned by rich landowners.

Peloponnesian War
/pel uh puh NEE zhuhn wor/ (n.)
(431 B.C.–404 B.C.)

a war in Ancient Greece between Athens and Sparta

See also: **Ancient Greece, Athens, battle, oligarchy, Sparta**

The **Peloponnesian War** was fought on land and at sea.

peninsula   /puh NIN suh luh/ (n.)

a piece of land surrounded by water on three sides

See also: **body of water, gulf, isthmus, landform, ocean**

Most of Florida is a **peninsula** because it is surrounded by the Atlantic Ocean and the Gulf of Mexico.

133

Penn, William
/pen, WIL yuhm/ (n.)
(1644–1718)

the founder of the colony
of Pennsylvania

See also: **colony, leader, Native Americans, negotiation, settler**

William Penn worked to make peace
between colonists and Native Americans.

per capita income
/pur KAP uh tuh IN kum/ (n.)

total income divided by number
of people

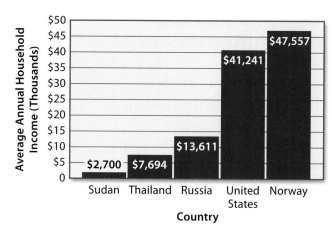

See also: **earnings, income, income tax, population, population density**

In 2010, Norway had the highest **per capita income**.

petition /puh TISH uhn/ (n.)
a document people sign
to show their support for
an idea or project

Don't Close **City Hospital!**
Sign the Petition!

Many people signed
the **petition** to keep
the hospital open
in their city.

See also: **ballot, candidate, city, civic participation, communication**

petroleum
/puh TROH lee uhm/ (n.)

a kind of oil

See also: **limited resource, non-renewable resource, ore, renewable resource, resource**

People drill into the ground to find **petroleum**. **Petroleum** is used to make gasoline.

pharaoh   /FA roh/ (n.)
a ruler of Ancient Egypt

See also: **ancient, civilization, Nile Valley, pyramid, ruler**

King Tutankhamen was a **pharaoh** of Egypt in the 1300s B.C.

physical feature
/FIZ uh kuhl FEE chur/ (n.)

a natural landform such as a mountain or river

Mt. Hood

Oregon

Crater Lake

See also: **body of water, landform, map, mountain, plateau, river**

Both Crater Lake and Mount Hood are **physical features** of Oregon.

135

Pico, Pio /PEE koh, PEE oh/ (n.)
(1801–1894)

the last governor of California when it was a part of Mexico

Pio Pico was governor of Mexican California from 1845 to 1846.

See also: **governor, Mexican-American War**

pilgrim /PIL gruhm/ (n.)

1. a person who travels to a holy place

Many Muslim **pilgrims** travel to the holy city of Mecca.

See also: **Islam, Muslim, religion, temple**

2. a person from England who traveled by boat to America in 1620

See also: **colony, Mayflower Compact, settlement, settler**

The **Pilgrims** traveled across the Atlantic Ocean on the *Mayflower*. They landed at Plymouth Rock in November, 1620.

pioneer /pī uh NEER/ (n.)

a person who is one of the first people from his or her group to live in a new area

Daniel Boone was a **pioneer**. He helped build the Wilderness Road from Virginia to Kentucky.

See also: **explore, frontier, settlement, settler**

plain   /playn/ (n.)

a flat area of land with few
or no trees

See also: **Great Plains, landform,
physical feature, plateau, prairie**

You can see for a long way on a **plain**.

plaintiff   /PLAYN tiff/ (n.)

a person in a court who blames
another person for a crime

See also: **court, defendant,
judge, jury, law**

The **plaintiff** blamed the defendant for stealing
his bike.

plantation   /plan TAY shuhn/ (n.)

a large farm, especially
in the South

See also: **agriculture; farming;
slave; slavery; South, the**

Many slaves lived and worked on a **plantation**.
Southern **plantations** often grew cotton and tobacco.

plateau /pla TOH/ (n.)

a high, flat piece of land

See also: **landform, mesa, physical feature, plain, prairie**

Canyonlands National Park is on a **plateau** in Utah. Some parts of the park are more than a mile above sea level.

Pledge of Allegiance
/plej uv uh LEE juhns/ (n.)

a statement of loyalty to the United States

See also: **allegiance, country, flag, nationalism, patriot**

In the United States, many students begin each school day by saying the **Pledge of Allegiance**.

Plessy v. Ferguson
/PLES ee VUR sus FUR guh sun/ (n.)

a Supreme Court ruling in 1896 that stated that segregation of races was legal

See also: ***Brown v. Board of Education,*** **equality, racism, segregation, Supreme Court**

The ***Plessy v. Ferguson*** decision kept African Americans in separate schools from whites.

policy /POL uh see/ (n.)

a plan of action by a government, company, or other organization

President Theodore Roosevelt introduced environmental **policies** to protect forests, wildlife, and natural resources.

See also: **foreign policy, government, natural resource, regulation, rule**

political cartoon
/puh LIT uh kuhl kar TOON/ (n.)

a drawing that gives an opinion about government

See also: **colony; Franklin, Benjamin; government; politics**

Benjamin Franklin drew a **political cartoon** to show that the U.S. colonies needed to stay united.

political party
/puh LIT uh kuhl PAR tee / (n.)

a group of people who work together to win control of a government

See also: **caucus, election, government, politics**

The United States has two major **political parties**.

139

political system
/puh LIT uh kuhl SIS tuhm/ (n.)

the way a government
is organized

Three Branches of Government

Legislative	Executive	Judicial
Congress	President	Courts

See also: **democracy, dictator,
government, monarchy, politics**

A democracy is one type of **political system**.

politics /POL uh tiks/ (n.)

the activities involved
in running a government

See also: **city council, civic participation,
government, political party,
political system**

Anyone can get involved in **politics**. Citizens can go
to meetings at City Hall and tell the mayor how to
make their city better.

pollution /puh LOO shuhn/ (n.)

something that makes air, land,
or water dirty

See also: **factory, legislation,
policy, regulation**

Smoke from factories is a cause of air **pollution**.

Pony Express
/POH nee ek SPRES/ (n.)
(1860–1861)

a method used to deliver mail between Missouri and California

See also: **Great Plains; pioneer; settler; transportation; West, the**

It took the **Pony Express** 10 days to deliver a letter from Missouri to California.

popular sovereignty
/POP yuh lur SOV ruhn tee/ (n.)

the idea that people have the power to choose their own government

See also: **democracy, election, government, leader, vote**

A democracy is based on **popular sovereignty**. The people vote for their leaders.

population
/pop yuh LAY shuhn/ (n.)

the number of people living in an area

See also: **census, demographic, inhabitant, population density, population growth**

Nevada
2.7 million

Utah
2.8 million

California
37.7 million

Arizona
6.5 million

California has a **population** of over 37 million people. The **populations** of Nevada, Utah, and Arizona are smaller.

population density
/pop yuh LAY shuhn DEN suh tee/ (n.)

the number of people living
in a certain amount of space

New York City has a high **population density**. There
are about 27,000 people living in every square mile.

---

population growth
/pop yuh LAY shuhn grohth/ (n.)

increase in the number of people
living in a certain area

The **population growth** in the United States was very
high in the 20th century. The population grew from
76 million people in 1900 to 281 million people in 2000.

---

port /port/ (n.)

a place where ships load
and unload goods

New Orleans has one of the largest **ports**
in the United States.

poverty /POV ur tee/ (n.)

a lack of money or
other resources

Soup kitchens give free food to people living
in **poverty**.

See also: **famine, limited resource,
money, resource, unemployment**

power /POW ur/ (n.)

the authority of a person
to do something

The president of the
United States has the
power of veto.

See also: **authority, federal government,
government, popular sovereignty, veto**

prairie /PRAIR ee/ (n.)

a large, flat area of land that is
covered with grass

Prairie covers parts of the Midwest in the
United States.

See also: **Great Plains, landform,
plain, region**

Preamble of the United States Constitution
/PREE am buhl uv THuh yoo NĪ tid stayts kon stuh TOO shuhn/ (n.)

a statement that begins the U.S. Constitution

See also: **American Revolution, Bill of Rights, constitution, Declaration of Independence, Founders**

We the People of the United States, in order to form a more perfect union, establish justice, insure domestic tranquility, provide for the common defense, promote the general welfare, and secure the blessings of liberty toourselves and our posterity, do ordain and establish this Constitution for the United States of America.

The **Preamble of the United States Constitution** tells what the constitution does and why the Founders wrote it.

---

precedent /PRES uh duhnt/ (n.)
an example that is followed

See also: *Brown v. Board of Education,* **court, law, Supreme Court**

The Supreme Court decision on *Brown v. Board of Education* set a **precedent**. It made segregated schools illegal.

---

predict /pri DIKT/ (v.)
to make a guess about what will happen in the future

New York, NY
Tomorrow's weather
72°
Cloudy

See also: **election, investment, stock, stock market**

The job of a meteorologist is to study and **predict** the weather.

prehistoric
/pree hi STOR ik/ (adj.)

having to do with a time before history was written

See also: **age, ancient, artifact, culture, tool**

Prehistoric people in the Stone Age made tools from stone and bones.

prejudice /PREJ uh dis/ (n.)

an unfair opinion about someone

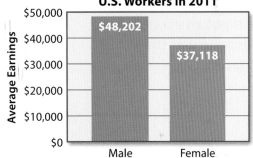

Average Earnings for Full-time U.S. Workers in 2011

$48,202 — Male

$37,118 — Female

See also: **bias, discrimination, equality, Jim Crow laws, racism**

Some employers have a **prejudice** against women. In 2011, many women were paid less than men for working full-time jobs.

president /PREZ uh duhnt/ (n.)

the person in charge of the executive branch of the U.S. government

Barack Obama became the 44th **president** of the United States in 2009.

See also: **authority, branch of government, Cabinet, election, government**

price /prīs/ (n.)

the cost of an item or service

See also: **cost, goods, inflation, money, profit**

The smartphone's **price** is $199.

primary source

/PRĪ mer ee SORS/ (n.)

a retelling of an event by a person who was there at that time

See also: **artifact, secondary source, soldier, testimony**

A soldier's diary is a **primary source**. People in the future can study the diary to learn what happened in the war.

prime meridian

/prīm muh RID ee uhn/ (n.)

an imaginary line that runs from the North Pole to the South Pole

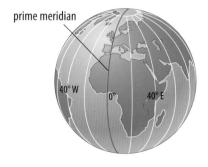

prime meridian

40° W   0°   40° E

See also: **globe, latitude line, longitude line, meridian, parallel**

The **prime meridian** runs through Greenwich, England. It divides Earth into two hemispheres.

146

Prime Minister
/prīm MIN uh stur/ (n.)

a person in some countries who leads the government

Stephen Harper became **Prime Minister** of Canada in 2006.

See also: **country, government, leader, political party, president**

---

principle   /PRIN suh puhl/ (n.)

a belief or rule about what is right

Many people believe in the **principle** that all men and women are equal.

See also: **bias, Bill of Rights, freedom, right**

---

printing press
/PRIN ting pres/ (n.)

a machine that can make many paper goods such as books, magazines, and newspapers

Johannes Gutenberg built the first **printing press** in the mid-1400s.

See also: **innovation, invention, manufacturing, mass production, media**

product /PROD uhkt/ (n.)

something that is made

See also: **business, factory, goods, manufacturing, productivity**

A **product** is a physical object. Soup, cars, and books are **products**.

productivity
/pro duk TIV uh tee/ (n.)

the ability to make goods quickly

American workers have good **productivity**. They can make goods fast and at low cost.

See also: **factory, goods, labor, manufacturing, workforce**

profit /PROF it/ (n.)

the money earned through business activity

Earned: $30
Spent: − $10
Profit: $20

See also: **business, cost, economy, money**

The students made $30 at their bake sale, but spent $10 on supplies. The students made a $20 **profit**.

progressive /pruh GRES iv/ (n.)

a person who supports improving policies through change

President Theodore Roosevelt was a **progressive**. He was one of the first presidents to introduce laws to protect the environment.

See also: **government, policy, politics, president, social reform**

Prohibition
/proh uh BISH uhn/ (n.)
(1919–1933)

a period of time in the United States when it was illegal to make, sell, or buy alcohol

See also: **government, law, legislation, regulation**

Police officers would dump out any alcohol they found during **Prohibition**.

propaganda
/prop uh GAN duh/ (n.)

one-sided information that is given to people to make them support a goal, an opinion, or a government

During World War I, the U.S. government printed **propaganda** to encourage men to join the military.

See also: **government, military, policy, World War I**

149

prosecutor
/PROS uh kyoo tur/ (n.)

a lawyer who starts and leads
a court case against a person

The job of a **prosecutor** is to prove to a judge and jury that a defendant is guilty of a crime.

See also: **court, defendant, government, law, plaintiff**

province /PROV ins/ (n.)

a part of a country with its own local government

See also: **country, government, local, state**

A **province** is like a state. Ontario is a **province** in Canada.

public service
/PUB lik SUR vis/ (n.)

a job or career in government

See also: **government, governor, president, representative, senator**

Bill Clinton has been the president of the United States and a governor. He has spent much of his life in **public service**.

pueblo /PWEB loh/ (n.)

a Native American building in the Southwest made of stone and mud

A **pueblo** was large and had different floors. Different families would live together in one **pueblo**.

Puritan /PYUR uh tuhn/ (n.)

one of a group of Christians from England who came to live in America in the 1600s

Many **Puritans** settled in Massachusetts. Religion played a very important role in their lives.

pyramid /PEER uh mid/ (n.)

a large triangular building used as a tomb or temple in Ancient Egypt

The Great **Pyramid** of Giza was built in Egypt around 2550 B.C.

Qq

queen /kween/ (n.)
a female ruler of a monarchy

Elizabeth I was a **queen** of England. She ruled England from 1558 to 1603.

See also: **king, monarchy**

Rr

racism /RAY siz uhm/ (n.)
the belief that one race is better than another

See also: **civil rights, discrimination, equality, prejudice**

In 1947, Jackie Robinson overcame **racism** in baseball. He became the first African American to play in a national league.

railroad /RAYL rohd/ (n.)
a system of trains, tracks, and stations

See also: **commerce, invention, transcontinental railroad, transportation**

A **railroad** moves people and goods across the country.

ranch /ranch/ (n.)

a business that raises
large farm animals

See also: **agriculture, farm,
labor, livestock**

King **Ranch** in Texas is one of the largest **ranches**
in the world. It raises cattle and horses.

ratify /RAT uh fi/ (v.)

to give formal approval
of a decision

See also: **amendment, constitution,
Senate, treaty**

An important job of the U.S. Senate is to **ratify**
agreements between countries. In 1803, the Senate
ratified the Louisiana Purchase from France.

raw material
/raw muh TEER ee uhl/ (n.)

a part of nature that people
can use

See also: **manufacturing, natural resource,
non-renewable resource, ore, resource**

Cotton is a **raw material**. We use it to make socks
and other clothes.

153

recession /ri SESH uhn/ (n.)

a period of at least nine months when businesses do not make money

See also: **business, deflation, economy, inflation, unemployment**

Many businesses close during a **recession**.

Reconstruction
/ree kuhn STRUK shuhn/ (n.)
(1865–1877)

a period of time after the U.S. Civil War when the U.S. government controlled former Confederate states

See also: **civil war; Confederacy; representative; senator; Union, the**

The first African American senator and representatives were chosen during **Reconstruction**.

recycle /ree SĪ kuhl/ (v.)

to keep used objects and use them again

See also: **business, limited resource, non-renewable resource, renewable resource, resource**

People **recycle** old bottles to be used again.

refugee   /REF yuh jee/ (n.)

a person who leaves his or her country in a time of danger

See also: **civil war, displace, drought, famine, homeland**

In 2011, Syrian **refugees** left their country to escape a civil war.

region   /REE juhn/ (n.)

a part of a country or of the world

Mountain West
Midwest
Northeast
Pacific West
Southwest
South

See also: **Central America, Fertile Crescent, Great Plains, Middle East, Nile Valley**

The six main **regions** of the United States are the Northeast, South, Southwest, Midwest, Mountain West, and Pacific West.

regulation
/reg yuh LAY shuhn/ (n.)

an official rule

See also: **bill, government, legislation, restriction**

Many cities have a **regulation** that requires everyone to wear a helmet when riding a bicycle.

relative location
/REL uh tiv loh KAY shuhn/ (n.)

a way to describe where a place is by using other places

See also: **absolute location, cardinal direction, intermediate direction, location, map**

Mexico can be used to describe the United States' **relative location**. The U.S. is north of Mexico.

religion /ri LIJ uhn/ (n.)

a set of beliefs and practices used to worship a god or gods

See also: **Buddhism, Christianity, Hinduism, Islam, Judaism**

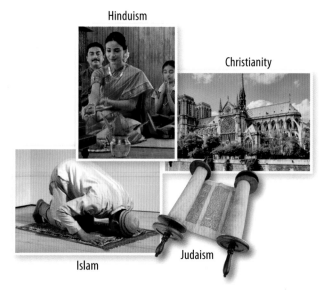

Hinduism

Christianity

Judaism

Islam

People practice many different **religions** around the world.

Renaissance
/ren uh SAHNS/ (n.)
(1300s–1600s)

a time period in Europe when people used ideas from ancient Greece and Rome

See also: **age, Ancient Greece, Ancient Rome, culture, movement**

Leonardo Da Vinci painted the famous Mona Lisa during the **Renaissance**.

renewable resource
/ri NOO uh buhl REE sors/ (n.)

a part of nature that people can use that can never run out

See also: **limited resource, non-renewable resource, raw material, resource**

Wind is a **renewable resource** that can be used to make electricity.

representative
/rep ri ZEN tuh tiv/ (n.)

a member of the House of Representatives

See also: **Capitol, the; Congress; democracy; election; House of Representatives**

All of the state **representatives** meet in Washington, D.C. to discuss laws and vote on bills.

republic   /ri PUB lik/ (n.)

a country where people choose the government and the leader

See also: **democracy, government, monarchy, oligarchy, political system**

The United States is a **republic**. The people of the United States vote in an election to choose their president.

reservation
/rez ur VAY shuhn/ (n.)

an area of land that is kept separate for Native Americans

See also: **government, Indian Removal Act, Indian Territory, Native Americans, Trail of Tears**

North Carolina has a large Cherokee **reservation**. A **reservation** has its own government.

---

reservoir   /REZ ur vwar/ (n.)

a pond or lake used to collect and store water

See also: **aqueduct, body of water, canal, irrigation, regulation**

People who live in a city or town depend on a **reservoir** for their water.

---

resource   /REE sors/ (n.)

a part of nature that a person, group, or country has and can use

See also: **limited resource, natural resource, non-renewable resource, ore, renewable resource**

Resources used in the United States include trees, water, and oil.

responsibility
/ri spon suh BIL uh tee/ (n.)

a duty a person is expected to do

A judge has the **responsibility** to be fair when deciding a case.

See also: **jury, right, role, service, volunteer**

restriction   /ri STRIK shuhn/ (n.)

a rule or law that sets limits

See also: **embargo, law, Prohibition, regulation, sanction**

Some states have **restrictions** on cell phone use while driving.

revenue   /REV uh noo/ (n.)

money that is collected by a person, business, or government

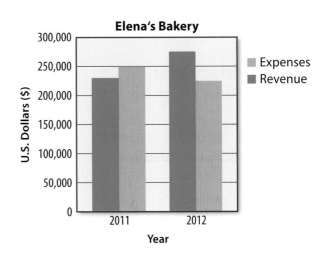

The bakery made a profit in 2012 because its **revenue** was greater than its expenses.

See also: **earnings, economy, income, profit, tax**

revolution
/rev uh LOO shuhn/ (n.)

1. a fight by people to end the rule of one government and start a new government

See also: **American Revolution, coup, French Revolution, Great Britain, Revolutionary War**

The American **Revolution** was a fight by American colonists against Great Britain.

2. a sudden or very large change

See also: **assembly line, Industrial Revolution, invention, mass production, transportation**

The steam engine brought about a **revolution** in technology and transportation.

Revolutionary War
/rev uh LOO shuh ner ee wor/ (n.)
(1775–1783)

the war between the American colonies and Great Britain (also known as the American Revolution)

George Washington led the American troops in the **Revolutionary War**. They fought for independence from Great Britain.

See also: **American Revolution, colony, Great Britain, independence, revolution**

right /rīt/ (n.)

what a person is allowed to do by law

See also: **civil right, First Amendment, individual right, states' rights**

Citizens have the **right** to vote in the United States.

risk /risk/ (n.)

the chance of something bad happening

See also: **capitalism, entrepreneur, investment, profit**

People who open a business take a **risk**. There is a chance the business might lose money.

river /RIV ur/ (n.)

a long, wide body of water that flows into the ocean

See also: **body of water, Mississippi River, tributary, waterway**

Minnesota

Mississippi River

Gulf of Mexico

The longest **river** in North America is the Mississippi. It flows from northern Minnesota to the Gulf of Mexico.

Rocky Mountains

/ROK ee MOWN tuhnz/ (n.)

the largest mountain range
in North America

See also: **landform, landmark, mountain,
mountain range, physical feature**

The **Rocky Mountains** are more than 3,000 miles
long. They stretch from New Mexico to British
Columbia, Canada.

---

role /rohl/ (n.)

what a person does during
a specific situation

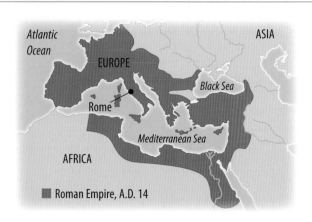

See also: **law, occupation, responsibility**

A paramedic's **role** is to give emergency care
to a sick or hurt person.

Roman Empire

/ROH muhn EM pīr/ (n.)
(27 B.C.–A.D. 476)

a large group of territories
ruled by Ancient Rome

See also: **ancient, Ancient Greece,
Ancient Rome, empire, territory**

The **Roman Empire** included regions in Europe,
Africa, and Asia.

Roman Republic
/ROH muhn ri PUB lik/ (n.)
(509 B.C.–27 B.C.)

a time in Ancient Rome when
people chose the leader
of their government

See also: **Ancient Rome,
checks and balances, democracy,
government, republic**

The **Roman Republic** is a model for democratic
governments today.

rule /rool/ (n.)

a statement that tells people
what they must or must not do

Class Rules
1. Raise your hand.

2. Listen when others
   are talking.

3. Take turns.

See also: **authority, law, regulation**

School **rules** help students to focus and learn.

rural /RUR uhl/ (adj.)
related to the country

See also: **agriculture, community,
crop, farming, urban**

Most farmers live in **rural** places.

Ss

Sacagawea
/sak uh juh WEE uh/ (n.)
(c. 1788–1812)

a Native American woman who helped Lewis and Clark explore the West from 1804 to 1806

See also: **expedition; Lewis and Clark; Louisiana Purchase; Native Americans; West, the**

Sacagawea helped Lewis and Clark find food that was safe to eat in the new U.S. territory.

---

sales tax /saylz taks/ (n.)

an amount of money that is added to the price of a good or service

See also: **consumer, cost, income tax, price, tax**

Tom's T-Shirts
123 Bellway Dr.
Chicago, IL 60606

Items
1 shirt–(1@10) $10.00
Sales Tax (9.5%) $0.95
TOTAL $10.95

Customer copy

The price of the T-shirt is $10.00. The **sales tax** is 95 cents. The total cost of the T-shirt is $10.95.

---

sanction /SANGK shuhn/ (n.)

an action that is taken by one country against another country

See also: **conflict, country, embargo, World War II**

The U.S. government put **sanctions** on trade with Japan in 1941. U.S. companies were not allowed to sell steel or oil to Japan.

savanna /suh VAN uh/ (n.)

type of grassland found in warm areas of the world

The continent of Africa has many large **savannas**. **Savannas** attract animals that eat grass.

See also: **coastal plain, Great Plains, physical feature, plain, prairie**

Scandinavia

/skan duh NAY vee uh/ (n.)

a region of Northern Europe

Scandinavia includes the countries of Denmark, Sweden, Norway, Finland, and Iceland.

See also: **country, map, region**

---

scarcity /SKAIR suh tee/ (n.)

an amount that is not enough

Over one billion people around the world live in areas where there is a **scarcity** of water.

See also: **limited resource, natural resource, non-renewable resource, renewable resource, surplus**

secede /si SEED/ (v.)

to leave a group such as a country or government

See also: **civil war; Confederacy; government; state; Union, the**

Eleven states **seceded** from the Union during the U.S. Civil War.

secondary source
/SEK uhn der ee sors/ (n.)

a retelling of an event by a person who was not there

See also: **biography, history, primary source**

A textbook is a **secondary source** of information.

sectionalism
/SEK shuh nuh liz uhm/ (n.)

the act of caring strongly about the interests of one's own group or region

Sectionalism in the United States, 1863

- Union States
- Border States
- Seceded States

See also: **civil war, region, secede, slavery, states' rights**

The issue of slavery caused **sectionalism** in the United States in the mid-1800s. **Sectionalism** led the South to secede from the Union in 1860.

segregation

/seg ruh GAY shuhn/ (n.)

the act of keeping different groups of people apart

See also: **civil war, Jim Crow laws, racism, Reconstruction**

After the U.S. Civil War, racial **segregation** was common in the South until the 1960s.

---

self-government

/self GUHV urn muhnt/ (n.)

a system of government in which citizens rule themselves

See also: **autonomy, citizen, democracy, election, government**

A city council is based on **self-government**. People who live in the city can run for office.

---

self-sufficient

/self suh FISH uhnt/ (adj.)

able to survive with little help from others

See also: **adapt, Great Plains, independence, pioneer, trade**

Pioneer families had to be **self-sufficient**. They lived far away from cities and towns.

167

Senate /SEN it/ (n.)

one part of Congress
that makes laws

See also: **Congress,
House of Representatives,
legislation, senator, state**

There are 100 senators in the U.S. **Senate**. Each state
elects two senators to represent it.

senator /SEN uh tur/ (n.)

a member of the Senate

Senator Hattie
Caraway of Arkansas
was the first woman
to be elected to
the U.S. Senate on
January 12, 1932.

See also: **bill, Congress,
House of Representatives,
legislation, Senate**

separation of powers
/sep uh RAY shuhn uv POW urz/ (n.)

a way for each branch
of government to have
a fair balance of power

Legislative

Executive   Judicial

See also: **branch of government, checks
and balances, constitution, power**

The writers of the U.S. Constitution included the
separation of powers in the Constitution. They did
not want government leaders to become too powerful.

service /SUR vis/ (n.)

work that gives people the help they need or want

See also: **consumer, goods, industry, institution, need**

Doctors offer medical **services** to their patients.

settlement /SET uhl muhnt/ (n.)

a place where many people build homes to live

See also: **colony, community, pilgrim, pioneer, settler**

The English built the first permanent North American **settlement** at Jamestown in 1607.

settler /SET lur/ (n.)

a person who goes to live in an area where there are few or no people

See also: **colony, community, pilgrim, pioneer, settlement**

English **settlers** founded Plymouth in 1620.

sharecropping
/SHAIR krop ing/ (n.)

a way in which a landowner can rent land to farmers

See also: **agriculture, civil war, crop, farming, subsistence level**

Sharecropping was common after the U.S. Civil War. The farmers paid the landowner rent with a part of their crop.

shelter /SHEL tur/ (n.)

a place that protects from danger or bad weather

See also: **adapt, harbor, hunter-gatherer**

Caves often served as **shelter** for hunter-gatherers.

Shinto /SHIN toh/ (n.)

a religion that is common in Japan

See also: **Buddhism, Hinduism, religion, shrine, Sikhism**

The Torii Gate is a symbol of the **Shinto** religion.

shogun /SHOH gun/ (n.)

a military leader of Japan who had more power than the emperor

The first **shogun** of Japan was Minamoto Yoritomo. **Shoguns** ruled Japan from 1192 to 1867.

See also: **emperor, leader, military**

shrine /shrīn/ (n.)

a special place that is important to people for religious reasons

See also: **Buddhism, Hinduism, religion, Shinto, Sikhism**

A Buddhist **shrine** usually contains a statue of the Buddha and candles.

siege /seej/ (n.)

when an army surrounds a fortress or a town so that no one can enter or leave

See also: **battle, blockade, Middle Ages, military, surrender**

During the Middle Ages, an army would try to take control of a castle by **siege**. The **siege** could last for months or years.

Sikhism /SEEK iz uhm/ (n.)

a religion common in some parts of India

See also: **Buddhism, Hinduism, religion, Shinto, temple**

The Golden Temple is the main temple of **Sikhism**. It was built in 1604.

Silk Road /silk rohd/ (n.)

a route for buying and selling goods that connected China to Europe

See also: **city, commerce, goods, trade, trade route**

Silk Road, A.D. 100

The **Silk Road** stretched for 4,000 miles. Major cities developed on the busy trade route.

slave /slayv/ (n.)

a person with no freedom who is forced to work for no pay

See also: **civil war, Confederacy, slavery, slave state**

Slaves were considered property, not people. They were sold, and families were often separated.

slavery /SLAY vur ee/ (n.)

owning other people and forcing them to work for no pay

See also: **civil war; Confederacy; Emancipation Proclamation; slave; South, the**

Slavery was common on cotton plantations in the South.

slave state /slayv stayt/ (n.)

a U.S. state that allowed slavery until the end of the U.S. Civil War

See also: **civil war, Confederacy, Emancipation Proclamation, free state, slavery**

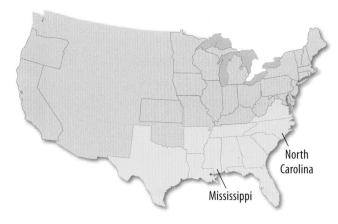

Mississippi and North Carolina were once **slave states**.

Smith, John /smith, jon/ (n.)
(1580–1631)

one of the first leaders of the Jamestown settlement

John Smith and about 100 other settlers started the Jamestown Settlement in 1607.

See also: **colony, leader, pioneer, settlement, settler**

social class
/SOH shuhl klas/ (n.)

a group of people who share similar lifestyles in society

See also: **farming, merchant, peasant, society**

During the Middle Ages, peasants and landowners belonged to different **social classes**. Peasants were in a lower **social class** than the landowners.

socialism
/SOH shuh liz uhm/ (n.)

an economic system in which many businesses are owned and run by the government

See also: **capitalism, communism, economy, government, industry**

The government of Vietnam controls the majority of the businesses in the country. The economy of Vietnam is an example of **socialism**.

social reform
/SOH shuhl ree FORM/ (n.)

a series of actions taken to make people's lives better

See also: **civic participation, community, leader, public service, volunteer**

Lillian Wald was a leader of **social reform** in the early 1900s. She started educational programs in poor communities.

Social Security
/SOH shuhl si KYUR uh tee/ (n.)
a government program that gives money to people of a certain age

See also: **benefit, government, Great Depression, social reform, welfare**

A U.S. citizen can receive **Social Security** when he or she can no longer work.

society /suh SĪ uh tee/ (n.)
a group of people who live in the same place and share the same culture

See also: **civilization, community, culture, Industrial Revolution, institution**

The Industrial Revolution changed American **society**. People left the countryside to live in busy, crowded cities.

soldier /SOL jur/ (n.)
a person who prepares to fight or fights in a war

The U.S. Civil War divided families. **Soldiers** from the same family fought on opposite sides.

See also: **battle, civil war, conflict, Continental Army, military**

source /sors/ (n.)

the place where a river begins

The Sierra Nevada mountain range is the **source** of many of California's rivers.

See also: **mountain range, river, tributary, waterway**

South, the /sowth, тнuh/ (n.)

an area in the southeastern part of the United States

See also: **civil war; Confederacy; North, the; region; secede**

Many states in **the South** seceded during the U.S. Civil War.

Southwest, the
/sowth WEST, тнuh/ (n.)

a region of the United States

See also: **canyon, region, Rocky Mountains**

The **Southwest** is the driest region of the United States.

Sparta /SPAR tuh/ (n.)

an ancient Greek city-state

See also: **ancient, Ancient Greece, Athens, city-state, Peloponnesian War**

Sparta went to war with Athens from 431 B.C. to 404 B.C. This war became known as the Peloponnesian War.

specialize /SPESH uh līz/ (v.)

to learn a lot about one subject

See also: **consumer, goods, industry, occupation, service**

Some doctors **specialize** in one area of medicine. A pediatrician **specializes** in the health of children.

Stamp Act /stamp akt/ (n.)

a law passed by the British in 1765 that taxed all official documents in the American colonies

See also: **Boston Tea Party, colony, law, Revolutionary War, tax**

The **Stamp Act** required that all printed materials, such as newspapers, carry an official stamp showing that a tax had been paid.

177

standard of living

/STAN durd uv LIV ing/ (n.)

the amount of money and comfort a person, group, or country has in daily life

See also: **cost, income, money, need, want**

The number of years spent in school is one way to measure **standard of living**.

---

staple /STAY puhl/ (n.)

a food that is eaten often

Rice is a **staple**. It is eaten in many countries around the world.

See also: **adapt, agrarian, agriculture, product**

---

state /stayt/ (n.)

a part of a country that has its own government and can make some of its own laws

CALIFORNIA

Sacramento

See also: **city, community, country, county, region**

The **state** of California passed its own environmental laws in 1970 to protect its lands, air, waters, and communities.

states' rights /stayts rīts/ (n.)

the powers that a state
government has

See also: **Bill of Rights, constitution,
federal government, government, local**

States' rights are guaranteed in the Bill of Rights.
States have the right to run their own schools.

Statue of Liberty
/**STACH oo uv LIB ur tee**/ (n.)

a large, metal figure in New York
that is a symbol of freedom
in the United States

The **Statue of Liberty**
was a gift from France.
It honors United States
immigrants.

See also: **flag, freedom,
immigrant, liberty**

steamboat /STEEM boht/ (n.)

a boat that uses an engine
powered by steam

See also: **goods, industry,
invention, river, transportation**

Robert Fulton built the first **steamboat** in 1807.
It changed how people traveled and how goods
were shipped.

stock /stok/ (n.)

a share in a company or business that someone can buy

See also: **free enterprise, investment, stockholder, stock market**

If you buy **stock** in a successful company, you can earn a lot of money.

stockholder
/STOK hohl dur/ (n.)

a person who owns at least one share in a company

See also: **free enterprise, money, stock, stock market**

Some **stockholders** must meet at least once a year to vote on what their company is going to do in the future.

stock market
/STOK mar kit/ (n.)

where people buy and sell stocks in companies

People buy and sell stocks on the **stock market**. The New York Stock Exchange is the largest of all U.S. **stock markets**.

See also: **free enterprise, investment, stock, stockholder**

strike /strīk/ (n.)

a period of time when employees stop working until specific demands are met

See also: **compromise, labor union, right, workforce**

Employees in a labor union will sometimes go on **strike** if their company does not pay them enough money for their work.

subsidy /SUB suh dee/ (n.)

money that is paid by the government to regulate the cost of goods and services

See also: **farming, goods, government, price, service**

The U.S. government can give a **subsidy** to farmers to help keep the prices of fruits and vegetables low.

subsistence level
/suhb SIS tuhns LEV uhl/ (n.)

the lowest amount of money or food needed to live

See also: **hunter-gatherer, money, need, peasant, poverty**

Many people in the world live at the **subsistence level**. They must find or farm their own food every day in order to survive.

suburb /SUB urb/ (n.)

a community near a large city

See also: **city, community, country, rural, urban**

Levittown, New York is a **suburb** of New York City. It was one of the first modern **suburbs** in the United States.

suffrage /SUF rij/ (n.)

the right to vote

See also: **Anthony, Susan B.; Nineteenth Amendment; vote; women's suffrage movement**

Women gained **suffrage** in the United States in 1920.

superpower
/SOO pur pow ur/ (n.)

a country with a lot of political and military strength or power

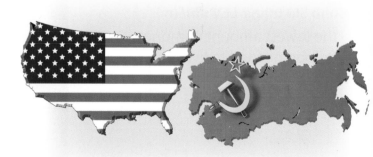

See also: **arms race; Cold War, the; military; power; U.S.S.R.**

The United States and the U.S.S.R. were **superpowers** during the Cold War.

supply and demand
/suh PLĪ end di MAND/ (n.)

the amount of an available product compared with the amount that people want to buy

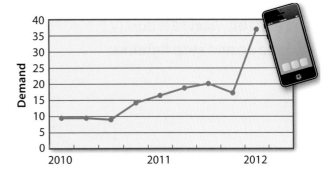

See also: **consumer, goods, scarcity, service, surplus**

The price of a product depends on **supply and demand**. When there is a high demand for smartphones, the price of smartphones goes up.

Supreme Court
/suh PREEM kort/ (n.)

the highest court in the United States

See also: **branch of government, Chief Justice, constitution, law, unconstitutional**

The national and state governments must follow the decisions of the **Supreme Court**.

surplus /SUR pluhs/ (n.)

an amount greater than what is needed or used

See also: **consumer, deflation, scarcity, supply and demand**

Prices fall when there is a **surplus** of products. If there is a **surplus** of cotton, the price of cotton goes down.

surrender /suh REN dur/ (v.)
to give up and stop fighting

See also: **Appomattox Court House, battle, civil war, siege, soldier**

General Lee went to the Appomattox Court House to **surrender** to General Grant on April 9, 1865.

synagogue /SIN uh gawg/ (n.)
a place of worship for followers of Judaism

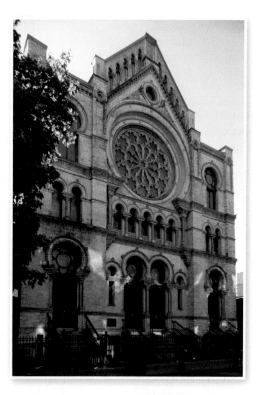

See also: **Judaism, monotheism, religion, temple**

The Eldridge Street **Synagogue** in New York City was built in 1887.

Tt

Taoism /DOW iz uhm/ (n.)

a religion especially common in China

See also: **Buddhism, religion, temple**

The Yin-Yang is a symbol of **Taoism**. It represents the balance between opposites such as light and dark.

---

tax /taks/ (n.)

money that a government collects to help pay for public services

Tom's T-Shirts
123 Bellway Dr.
Chicago, IL 60606
Items
1 shirt–(1@10) $10.00
Sales Tax (9.5%) $0.95
TOTAL $10.95

Customer copy

See also: **goods, government, income tax, public service, sales tax**

The sales **tax** on the T-shirt will go to the government to help pay for public services like schools and hospitals.

---

temple /TEM puhl/ (n.)

a building where people go to pray or hear someone talk about religion

See also: **Buddhism, church, mosque, religion, shrine**

People who follow Buddhism often go to **temples** to pray.

territorial expansion
/ter uh TOR ee uhl ek SPAN shuhn/ (n.)
   the addition of new land
   to a country

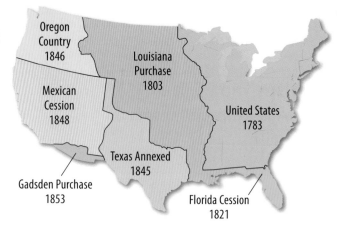

See also: **expansion, Louisiana Purchase, Manifest Destiny, territory**

1783 to 1853 was a period of **territorial expansion** in the United States.

---

territory /TER uh tor ee/ (n.)
   land that belongs to a country

See also: **government, Louisiana Purchase, Manifest Destiny, state, territorial expansion**

Puerto Rico is a **territory** of the United States.

---

terrorism /TER uh riz uhm/ (n.)
   the use of violence to scare
   people for political reasons

See also: **conflict, defense, national security**

Safety checks at an airport can help stop **terrorism**.

testimony /TES tuh moh nee/ (n.)

a public statement made by a person that states the truth

See also: **court, defendant, jury, law, prosecutor**

A witness in court must promise to tell the truth before giving a **testimony**.

textile /TEK stīl/ (n.)

any kind of cloth that is woven or knit

See also: **factory, industry, manufacturing, product**

Textiles are often made on machines in factories.

thematic map
/thee MAT ik map/ (n.)

a type of map that shows information specific to an area

Presidential Election 2008
■ Obama
■ McCain

See also: **election, geography, map, map key**

This **thematic map** shows how each state voted in the 2008 election.

187

theocracy /thee OK ruh see/ (n.)

a form of government
in which a country is ruled
by religious leaders

See also: **country, government,
Islam, leader, religion**

The country of Iran is a **theocracy**. It is ruled
by an Islamic leader.

---

timber /TIM bur/ (n.)

wood that is used for building

See also: **business, industry,
limited resource, resource**

Many houses in the United States are built with **timber**.

---

timeline /TĪM līn/ (n.)

a line with marks that shows
the order of important events
in the past

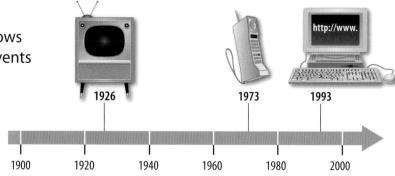

1926   1973   1993

1900   1920   1940   1960   1980   2000

See also: **A.D., B.C.,
chronology, history,
time period**

A **timeline** can show important events in history.
This **timeline** shows the invention of the television,
the cell phone, and the Internet.

time period
/TĪM peer ee uhd/ (n.)

an amount of time with a beginning and an end

Victorian Era

1825   1850   1875   1900   1925

See also: **A.D., age, B.C., era, timeline**

The Victorian Era was a **time period** from 1837 to 1901. This **time period** was named for Queen Victoria.

---

time zone /tīm zohn/ (n.)

an area of the world that has its own time

U.S. Time Zones

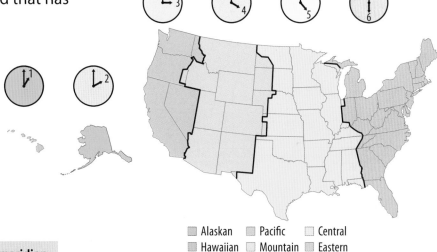

☐ Alaskan   ☐ Pacific   ☐ Central
☐ Hawaiian ☐ Mountain ☐ Eastern

See also: **longitude line, meridian, prime meridian, region**

There are six different **time zones** in the United States.

---

tool /tool/ (n.)

a device used to do a job

See also: **age, industry, invention, product**

A hammer is a type of **tool** used for building. The Internet is a type of **tool** used for finding information.

189

totalitarian
/to tahl uh TER ee uhn/ (adj.)

having complete control over the people of a country

See also: **autocrat, dictator, leader, power, U.S.S.R.**

Joseph Stalin was a **totalitarian** leader of the U.S.S.R. from 1941 until his death in 1953.

trade /trayd/ (n.)

the buying and selling of goods or services

See also: **barter, exchange, goods, industry, timber**

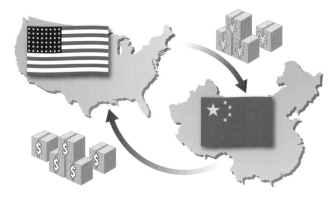

International **trade**, such as the **trade** between the United States and China, is an important part of the world economy.

trade-off /trayd of/ (n.)

a negative situation that must be accepted in return for a positive situation

See also: **barter, exchange, money, trade**

Marla's mother gave her money to go to the movies. The **trade-off** was that Marla had to help clean the yard.

trade route /trayd rowt/ (n.)

a path that people take
to buy and sell goods

See also: **Columbus, Christopher; merchant; Silk Road; trade; waterway**

Silk Road, A.D. 100

The Silk Road was a **trade route** that was used
from A.D. 1 to A.D. 1400.

---

trade wind /trayd wind/ (n.)

a constant movement of air
that blows in one direction

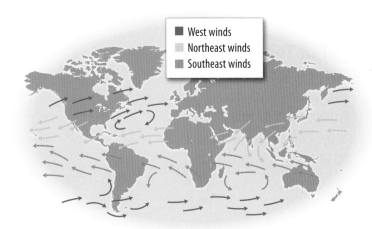

- West winds
- Northeast winds
- Southeast winds

See also: **canal, ocean, river, trade route, waterway**

Ships at sea will follow a **trade wind** to reach their
destination faster.

---

tradition /truh DISH uhn/ (n.)

a way of thinking or doing that
is passed down from adults
to children

See also: **culture, custom, norm, oral history, traditional economy**

It is a U.S. **tradition** for families to watch the fireworks
on the Fourth of July.

traditional economy
/truh DISH uh nuhl i KON uh mee/ (n.)

an economic system based
on necessary activities like
finding food

Some Inuit people in Canada have a
traditional economy.

See also: **agrarian, agriculture,
economy, farming, trade**

Trail of Tears
/trayl uv teerz/ (n.)

the journey taken by Native
Americans in the 1830s
after they were ordered
to leave their homeland

Arkansas River

Tennessee River

Mississippi River

■ Trail of Tears, 1838

Native Americans had to travel the **Trail of Tears**
from the Appalachian Mountains to the plains
of Oklahoma. It was a difficult journey, and
many Native Americans died.

See also: **Appalachian Mountains,
Indian Removal Act, Indian Territory,
Native Americans, reservation**

traitor /TRAY tur/ (n.)

someone who supports and
gives information to an enemy

Ethel and Julius Rosenberg were found guilty of
giving secret information to the U.S.S.R. Many people
believed that they were **traitors** to the United States.

See also: **allegiance; arms race; Cold War,
the; competition; treason**

transcontinental railroad
/tranz kon tuh NEN tuhl
RAYL rohd/ (n.)

a railroad that crosses a continent

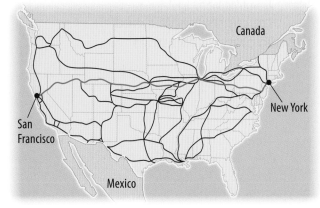

First Transcontinental Railroad, 1882

See also: **expansion, railroad, transportation**

The First **Transcontinental Railroad** helped make travel and shipping goods faster. It connected New York and San Francisco.

transportation
/tran spur TAY shuhn/ (n.)

a way of moving from one place to another

See also: **flat boat, Panama Canal, railroad, steamboat, transcontinental railroad**

Many people in New York City use public **transportation** such as buses and subways.

treason /TREE zuhn/ (n.)

a crime in which a person hurts his or her government or helps the country's enemies

See also: **allegiance, country, Revolutionary War, traitor**

Benedict Arnold committed **treason** during the Revolutionary War. He gave secret information to the British Army.

treaty   /TREE tee/ (n.)

a written agreement signed
by two or more countries

Mexico and the United States signed a **treaty** to stop
the Mexican-American War in 1848. Mexico agreed
to give its northern land to the United States.

See also: **agreement, armistice,
Mexican-American War,
Treaty of Paris**

Treaty of Paris
/TREE tee uv PAR is/ (n.)

a written agreement that ended
the American Revolution in 1783

See also: **agreement,
American Revolution,
country, treaty**

In the **Treaty of Paris**, Great Britain recognized
the United States as an independent country.

---

trench   /trench/ (n.)

a long hole dug in the ground
to protect soldiers

See also: **battle, civil war,
invasion, soldier**

In the past, soldiers would use a **trench** to protect
themselves from their enemies during war.

trend /trend/ (n.)

a new way of thinking or acting that many people follow

See also: **adapt, common, culture, movement, society**

One **trend** in education is the use of tablets in the classroom.

trial /TRĪ uhl/ (n.)

a meeting in court where a judge or jury reviews proof of a crime

See also: **court, defendant, judge, jury, lawyer**

A **trial** can decide if a person is innocent or guilty.

triangle trade
/TRĪ ang guhl trayd/ (n.)

trade between three ports or regions

Triangle Trade, 1752

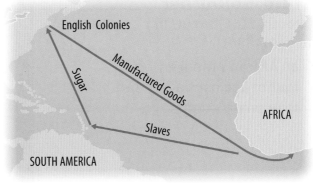

Goods from the colonies were traded for slaves in Africa in the **triangle trade** that took place in the 17th and 18th centuries.

See also: **colony, port, slave, trade**

tribe /trīb/ (n.)

a group of people who share the same language and traditions

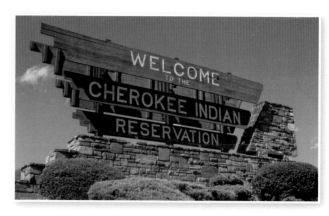

About 12,000 members of the Cherokee **tribe** live on the Cherokee Indian Reservation in North Carolina.

See also: **culture, custom, Native Americans, oral history, reservation**

tributary /TRIB yuh ter ee/ (n.)

a river that flows into a larger one

The Ohio River is a **tributary** of the Mississippi River.

See also: **body of water, canal, Mississippi River, river, waterway**

Truth, Sojourner
/trooth, SOH jurn ur/ (n.)
(c. 1797–1883)

an African American who fought against slavery and for women's rights

Sojourner Truth escaped from slavery in 1826.

See also: **Fifteenth Amendment, Nineteenth Amendment, slavery, suffrage, vote**

tsunami   /soo NAH mee/ (n.)

a giant wave caused by an
underwater earthquake

See also: **consequence, impact, ocean**

Many people
died in the
2011 **tsunami**
in Japan.

Tubman, Harriet
/TUB man, HAR ee et/ (n.)
(c. 1820-1913)

an escaped slave who helped
other slaves to escape

See also: **freedom; North, the; slave;
slavery; Underground Railroad**

Harriet Tubman escaped
from slavery in 1849. She
helped more than 300
slaves escape to freedom
in the North.

turning point
/TUR ning point/ (n.)

a time when an important
change takes place

See also: **American Revolution, civil war,
Declaration of Independence,
Emancipation Proclamation,
Louisiana Purchase**

The U.S. Civil War was a **turning point** in American
history. It ended slavery in the United States.

tyranny   /TIR uh nee/ (n.)

a government ruled by one
powerful and brutal person

See also: **autocrat; dictator; Hitler,
Adolf; oligarchy; totalitarian**

The Declaration of Independence stated that the king
of England wanted a **tyranny** in the colonies.

Uu

unalienable right
/un AY lyuh nuh buhl rīt/ (n.)

a right that cannot be given
or taken away

See also: **citizen, Declaration of Independence, liberty, right**

The writers of the Declaration of Independence
promised the American people an **unalienable
right** to liberty.

unconstitutional
/un kon stuh TOO shuh nuhl/ (adj.)

against the highest law
of a country

See also: *Brown v. Board of Education*, **civil right, constitution, integration, segregation**

In the 1954 case of *Brown v. Board of Education*,
the Supreme Court ruled that racial segregation
was **unconstitutional**.

Underground Railroad
/un dur GROWND RAYL rohd/ (n.)

a secret route used to help slaves
escape to the North before the
U.S. Civil War

See also: **civil war; North, the; slave; Tubman, Harriet**

Slaves who escaped on the **Underground Railroad**
were helped by people who believed slavery
was wrong.

unemployment
/un em PLOY muhnt/ (n.)

the state of having no job

See also: **economy, Great Depression, poverty, recession, workforce**

Unemployment reached very high levels during the Great Depression in the 1930s.

Union, the
/YOO nyuhn, THuh/ (n.)

the United States, especially the states that fought against the Confederate States during the U.S. Civil War

See also: **civil war; Confederacy; North, the; secede; state**

Union States

The Union fought against the Confederacy to keep the United States together.

Union of Soviet Socialist Republics (U.S.S.R.)
/YOO nyuhn uv SOH vee et SOH shuhl ist RI puh bliks/ (n.)
(1917–1991)

a powerful communist country in Asia

See also: **arms race; Cold War, the; communism; superpower**

U.S.S.R.

The **Union of Soviet Socialist Republics** had more land than any other country in history.

United Nations (UN)
/yoo NĪ tid NAY shuhnz/ (n.)

a group of representatives from 193 countries who work together for peace, health, and safety in the world

See also: **ambassador, development, diplomat, foreign policy, negotiation**

The **United Nations** sent peacekeepers to Haiti after the earthquake in 2010. The **UN** helped keep people safe and healthy.

unlimited government
/un LIM uh tid GUHV urn muhnt/ (n.)

a government in which the leader has total power and does not have to follow the same laws as the citizens

See also: **autocrat, dictator, fascism, right, tyranny**

German citizens had no rights or freedoms under the **unlimited government** of Nazi Germany.

urban /UR buhn/ (adj.)

related to a city

See also: **city, civilization, metropolitan area, population density, rural**

Urban areas include many tall buildings and people.

urbanization
/ur buh ni ZAY shuhn/ (n.)

turning land into part of a city

See also: **Industrial Revolution, natural resource, suburb, urban**

Many animals lose their homes because of **urbanization**.

veto /VEE toh/ (v.)

to say no to a bill passed
by lawmakers

The president can
veto bills passed
by Congress.

See also: **bill, checks and balances,
Congress, limited government, president**

Vietnam War

/vee et NAHM wor/ (n.)
(1954–1975)

a war between the countries
of North Vietnam and
South Vietnam

North Vietnam

Hanoi

South Vietnam

Saigon

In the **Vietnam War**,
the United States sent
soldiers to South Vietnam
to stop the communist
government of North
Vietnam from taking over
the country.

See also: **Cold War, the; communism;
foreign policy; soldier**

volunteer /vol uhn TEER/ (n.)

a person who does work
for no pay

See also: **civic participation,
public service, responsibility,
service**

Volunteers help people in need. These **volunteers**
are building a new home for a family.

201

vote /voht/ (v.)

to make a formal choice at an election or meeting

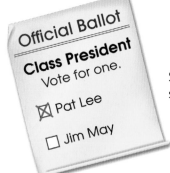

Students can **vote** to select a class president.

See also: **civic participation, election, Fifteenth Amendment, Nineteenth Amendment, suffrage**

Ww

want /wahnt/ (n.)

something one wishes for but does not need

Wants

See also: **budget, consumer, cost, expense, need**

Video games, cell phones, and amusement park tickets are all **wants**. Clothes, food, and shelter are needs.

War of 1812
/wor uv AY teen twelv/ (n.)
(1812–1815)

a war fought between the United States and Great Britain

See also: **Great Britain, invasion, territorial expansion**

During the **War of 1812**, British troops burned buildings in Washington, D.C. The White House was destroyed and had to be rebuilt.

waterway /WAW tur way/ (n.)

a river, lake, or ocean used
to move goods

See also: **body of water, canal,
goods, Mississippi River, river**

Minnesota

*Mississippi
River*

Gulf of Mexico

The Mississippi River
is a major trade
waterway in the
United States. This
waterway is used to
ship goods such as
coal, grain, and steel.

wealth /welth/ (n.)

the value of all money and
other resources

Natural Resources

Commerce

Education

Money

See also: **commerce,
gross domestic product, income,
money, per capita income**

A country's **wealth** can be measured by natural
resources, education, money, and commerce.

welfare /WEL fair/ (n.)

money and aid the government
gives to the poor

See also: **cost, earnings,
economy, income, poverty**

President Franklin D. Roosevelt signed the Social
Security Act during the Great Depression. Today, this
act continues to provide **welfare** to people in need.

203

West, the /west, THuh/ (n.)

the last part of the United States to be settled by Europeans

See also: **explore, frontier, Gold Rush, Lewis and Clark, pioneer**

U.S. President Thomas Jefferson sent Lewis and Clark to explore **the West**.

Western civilization
/WES turn siv uh luh ZAY shuhn/ (n.)

the modern culture of Europe and North America

See also: **Ancient Greece, Ancient Rome, civilization, culture, custom**

Western civilization began in Ancient Greece.

---

women's suffrage movement
/ WIM uhnz SUF rij MOOV muhnt/ (n.)
(1848–1920)

the fight for voting rights for women in the United States

See also: **amendment; Anthony, Susan B.; Nineteenth Amendment; suffrage; vote**

The **women's suffrage movement** succeeded in 1920 when women won the right to vote.

workforce /WERK fors/ (n.)

the total number of people in a country who are able to work

See also: **assembly line, industry, labor, productivity, unemployment**

In 2010, women made up 47% of the total **workforce** in the United States.

World War I
/**werld wor wun**/ (n.)
(1914-1918)

a conflict between the Central Powers and Allies

See also: **alliance, conflict, invasion, World War II**

The United States entered **World War I** in 1917 to protect passenger ships and trading goods from German attacks.

World War II
/**werld wor too**/ (n.)
(1939-1945)

a conflict between the Axis Powers and the Allied Powers

See also: **Allied Powers, Axis Powers, Nazi Party, U.S.S.R.**

World War II began on September 1, 1939 when Nazi Germany invaded Poland.

Power, Authority, and Governance

abolish
alliance
Allied Powers
ally
ambassador
amendment
annex
Anti-Federalist
armistice
arms race
Articles of Confederation
assassination
authority
autocrat
autonomy
Axis Powers
battle
bill
blockade
branch of government
Cabinet
campaign
candidate
capital
capitol
Capitol, the
central government
Central Powers
checks and balances
Chief Justice
city
city-state
civil war
colony
compromise
Confederacy
conflict
Congress
conquistador
constitution

Continental Army
country
county
coup
czar
defense
dictator
diplomat
Electoral College
emperor
empire
expansion
fascism
federal government
federalism
Federalist
felony
foreign policy
genocide
government
governor
House of Representatives
impeach
imperialism
institution
internment
invasion
isolationism
king
law
leader
legal
legislation
libel
limited government
majority
mayor
military
monarchy
nation

nationalism
national security
nation-state
neutral
oligarchy
ordinance
policy
political cartoon
political party
political system
politics
power
president
Prime Minister
propaganda
prosecutor
queen
representative
republic
sanction
secede
sectionalism
Senate
senator
separation of powers
shogun
siege
superpower
Supreme Court
surrender
territorial expansion
terrorism
theocracy
totalitarian
treason
treaty
tyranny
unlimited government
veto

Civic Ideals and Practices

agreement
allegiance
American Revolution
Anthony, Susan B.
appoint
assembly
ballot
benefit
Bill of Rights
Brown v. Board of Education
caucus
census
citizen
city council
civic participation
civil rights
common
community
court
debate
Declaration of
    Independence
defendant
democracy
Douglass, Frederick
due process
education
election
Emancipation Proclamation
Enlightenment
equality
evidence
exchange
Fifteenth Amendment
First Amendment
First Continental Congress
flag

Founders
Fourteenth Amendment
Franklin, Benjamin
freedom
Gettysburg Address
grand jury
guild
Hamilton, Alexander
Henry, Patrick
homeland
impartial
independence
individual right
integration
interpret
interview
issue
judge
jury
justice
King, Jr., Dr. Martin Luther
labor
labor union
liberty
local
Mayflower Compact
movement
naturalization
negotiation
Ninteenth Amendment
nominate
non-violence
occupation
ordinance
Paine, Thomas
Parks, Rosa
passive resistance

patriot
Penn, William
petition
plaintiff
Pledge of Allegiance
popular sovereignty
Preamble of the United
    States Constitution
precedent
principle
progressive
public service
ratify
Reconstruction
responsibility
Revolutionary War
right
role
rule
self-government
service
social reform
society
state
states' rights
Statue of Liberty
strike
suffrage
testimony
trial
unalienable right
unconstitutional
volunteer
vote
women's suffrage movement

Global Connections

allegiance
alliance
ally
ambassador
armistice
arms race
assimilate
battle
blockade
communication
compromise
country
diplomat

empire
expansion
explore
export
foreign policy
globe
immigrant
immigration
innovation
interdependence
invasion
invention

isolationism
media
multicultural
nation-state
neutral
OPEC
politics
superpower
territorial expansion
terrorism
trade route
treaty

Culture

Ancient Greece
Ancient Rome
architecture
artifact
assimilate
Aztec
biography
civilization

culture
custom
diversity
ethnicity
Hellenistic
Inca
Maya
multicultural

norm
political cartoon
religion
Renaissance
revolution
society
tradition
Western civilization

Individuals, Groups, and Institutions

adapt
adobe
agrarian
agriculture
ancestor
Ancient Greece
Ancient Rome
Anthony, Susan B.
apprentice
archaeologist
architecture

artifact
assimilate
Aztec
bias
biography
Buddhism
Christianity
church
civilization
Columbus, Christopher
communism

Confucianism
Confucius
conquistador
culture
custom
demographic
descendant
discrimination
displace
diversity
Douglass, Frederick

ethnicity
famine
farming
feudalism
Franklin, Benjamin
generation
Hamilton, Alexander
Hammurabi, Code of
Hellenistic
Henry, Patrick
hieroglyph
Hindu-Arabic numerals
Hinduism
Hitler, Adolf
hunter-gatherer
immigrant
immigration
Inca
indentured servant
inhabitant
Islam
Judaism
King, Jr., Dr. Martin Luther
Lafayette, Marquis de
Lewis and Clark
Loyalist
Maya

migrant worker
mission
monotheism
mosque
Mound Builders
multicultural
Muslim
Native Americans
Nazi Party
nomad
norm
Ottoman Empire
Paine, Thomas
Parks, Rosa
peasant
Peloponnesian War
Penn, William
pharaoh
Pico, Pio
pilgrim
pioneer
prejudice
pueblo
Puritan
racism
refugee
religion

reservation
Roman Empire
Roman Republic
Sacagawea
segregation
self-sufficient
settlement
settler
sharecropping
shelter
Shinto
shogun
shrine
Sikhism
slave
slavery
Smith, John
socialism
soldier
specialize
synagogue
Taoism
temple
traitor
Truth, Sojourner
Tubman, Harriet
United Nations (UN)

Places and Environments

absolute location
altitude
Appalachian Mountains
Appomattox Court House
Arctic
Athens
basin
Berlin Wall
body of water

border
boundary
canal
canyon
cape
capital
capitol
Capitol, the
cardinal direction

Central America
coast
coastal plain
compass
compass rose
continent
Continental Divide
demarcation line
drought

elevation
Eurasia
Fertile Crescent
Fort Sumter
free state
frontier
geography
globe
Great Britain
Great Plains
gulf
harbor
Indian Territory
inset map
intermediate direction
Iron Curtain
irrigation
isthmus
landform
landmark
latitude line
limited resource
location
longitude line
Louisiana Purchase
map
map key
map scale
Mason-Dixon Line
Mediterranean
meridian
mesa
metropolitan area
Middle East

migration
Mississippi River
mountain
mountain range
natural resource
Nile Valley
non-renewable resource
North, the
ocean
ore
Panama Canal
parallel
peninsula
petroleum
physical feature
plain
plantation
plateau
pollution
port
prairie
prime meridian
province
railroad
ranch
raw material
region
relative location
renewable resource
reservation
reservoir
resource
river
Rocky Mountains

rural
savanna
Scandinavia
settlement
shelter
Silk Road
slave state
source
South, the
Southwest, the
Sparta
staple
suburb
territory
thematic map
timber
tool
trade
trade route
trade wind
tradition
Trail of Tears
trench
tribe
tributary
tsunami
Underground Railroad
Union, the
Union of Soviet Socialist
    Republics (U.S.S.R.)
urban
waterway
West, the
Western civilization

Science, Technology, and Society

aqueduct
Bell, Alexander Graham
Carver, George Washington
communication
cotton gin
crop
crop rotation
Edison, Thomas
excavate
expedition
explore
flat boat
gold

Gold Rush
gunpowder
industrialization
Industrial Revolution
industry
infrastructure
innovation
invention
livestock
media
metropolitan area
Pony Express
population

population density
population growth
printing press
pyramid
recycle
steamboat
textile
transcontinental railroad
transportation
trend
urbanization

Production, Distribution, and Consumption

allocate
assembly line
bank
barter
bond
budget
business
capitalism
cash crop
commerce
compete
competition
consequence
consumer
cost
credit
crop

currency
debt
deficit
deflation
demand
development
distribution
earnings
economy
embargo
entrepreneur
expense
export
factory
Federal Reserve System
financial institution
free enterprise

goods
Great Depression
gross domestic product
    (GDP)
gross income
impact
import
income
income tax
inflation
interdependence
interest
investment
labor
labor union
loan
manufacturing

market economy
mass production
mercantilism
merchant
money
monopoly
need
OPEC
per capita income
port
poverty
power
price
product
productivity
profit

recession
regulation
restriction
revenue
risk
sales tax
sanction
scarcity
social class
Social Security
standard of living
stock
stockholder
stock market
strike

subsidy
subsistence level
supply and demand
surplus
tax
textile
trade-off
trade route
traditional economy
triangle trade
unemployment
want
wealth
welfare
workforce

Time, Continuity, and Change

A.D.
age
American Revolution
ancient
B.C.
Boston Massacre
Boston Tea Party
Brown v. Board of Education
century
chronology
Cold War, the
current
decade
Dred Scott v. Sandford
Enlightenment
era
French and Indian War
French Revolution
Fugitive Slave Act

Great Depression
history
Holocaust, the
Hundred Years War
Indian Removal Act
Industrial Revolution
Jim Crow laws
Korean Conflict
Manifest Destiny
Mexican-American War
Middle Ages
millennium (millenia)
Northwest Ordinance of 1787
oral history
Peloponnesian War
Plessy v. Ferguson
predict
prehistoric

primary source
Prohibition
Reconstruction
Renaissance
revolution
Revolutionary War
Roman Empire
Roman Republic
secondary source
Stamp Act
timeline
time period
time zone
Treaty of Paris
turning point
Vietnam War
War of 1812
World War I
World War II

George Washington

See also:
American Revolution, Continental Army, First Continental Congress

First President
1789–1797

Thomas Jefferson

See also:
Declaration of Independence, Louisiana Purchase

Third President
1801–1809

Abraham Lincoln

See also:
abolish, civil war, Emancipation Proclamation, Gettysburg Address

Sixteenth President
1861–1865

Ulysses S. Grant

See also:
Appomattox Court House, civil war, surrender

Eighteenth President
1869–1877

Theodore Roosevelt

See also:
policy, progressive

Twenty-Sixth President
1901–1909

Franklin D. Roosevelt

See also:
Great Depression, World War II

Thirty-Second President
1933–1945

Pacific
Ocean

WASHINGTON
★ Olympia

★ Salem
OREGON

Boise
★ IDAHO

MONTANA
Helena ★

NORTH
DAKOTA
Bismarck ★

SOUTH DAKOT.
Pierre ★

WYOMING

NEBRASKA

Cheyenne
★

★ Carson City
Sacramento ★
NEVADA

Salt Lake City
★
UTAH

★ Denver
COLORADO

KANSAS

CALIFORNIA

OKLAHOMA

ARIZONA

★ Santa Fe
Oklahoma City

NEW MEXICO

TEXAS

★ Phoenix

ALASKA

Austin
Juneau ★

MEXICO

Honolulu ★

HAWAII

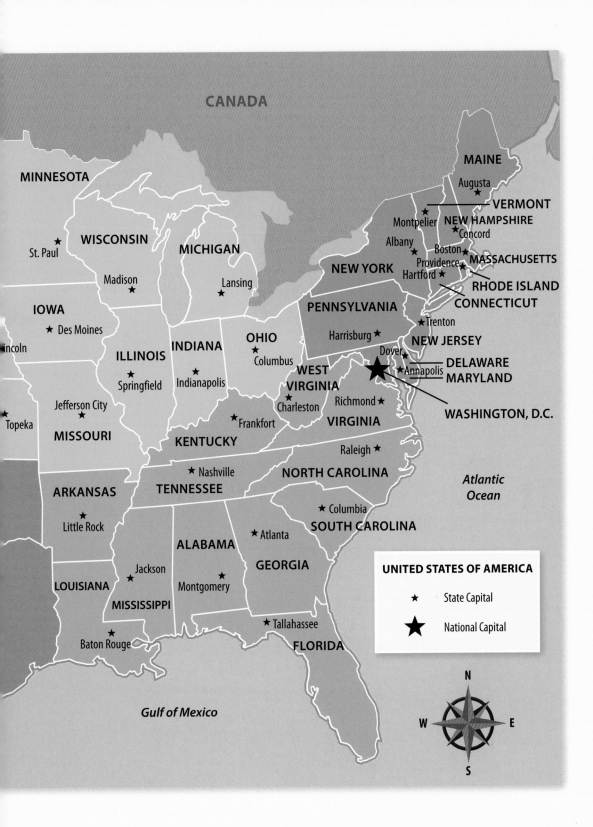

CANADA

MINNESOTA

MAINE

Augusta ★

VERMONT

Montpelier ★   NEW HAMPSHIRE
★ Concord

WISCONSIN

St. Paul ★

MICHIGAN

Madison ★

Lansing ★

Albany ★

NEW YORK

Boston
Providence ★
Hartford ★

MASSACHUSETTS

RHODE ISLAND

CONNECTICUT

IOWA

★ Des Moines

PENNSYLVANIA

Harrisburg ★

★ Trenton

NEW JERSEY

incoln

ILLINOIS

INDIANA

OHIO
★
Columbus

Dover
★

DELAWARE

Topeka

Springfield ★

Indianapolis ★

WEST
VIRGINIA

★ Annapolis

MARYLAND

Jefferson City
★

Charleston ★

Richmond ★

MISSOURI

Frankfort ★

VIRGINIA

WASHINGTON, D.C.

KENTUCKY

Raleigh ★

ARKANSAS

★ Nashville

NORTH CAROLINA

Little Rock ★

TENNESSEE

Atlantic
Ocean

★ Columbia

LOUISIANA

Jackson ★

ALABAMA

★ Atlanta

SOUTH CAROLINA

GEORGIA

MISSISSIPPI

Montgomery ★

UNITED STATES OF AMERICA

Baton Rouge ★

★ Tallahassee

★   State Capital

★   National Capital

FLORIDA

Gulf of Mexico

N

W   E

S

NORTH
AMERICA

Atlantic
Ocean

Pacific
Ocean

SOUTH
AMERICA

N

W   E

S

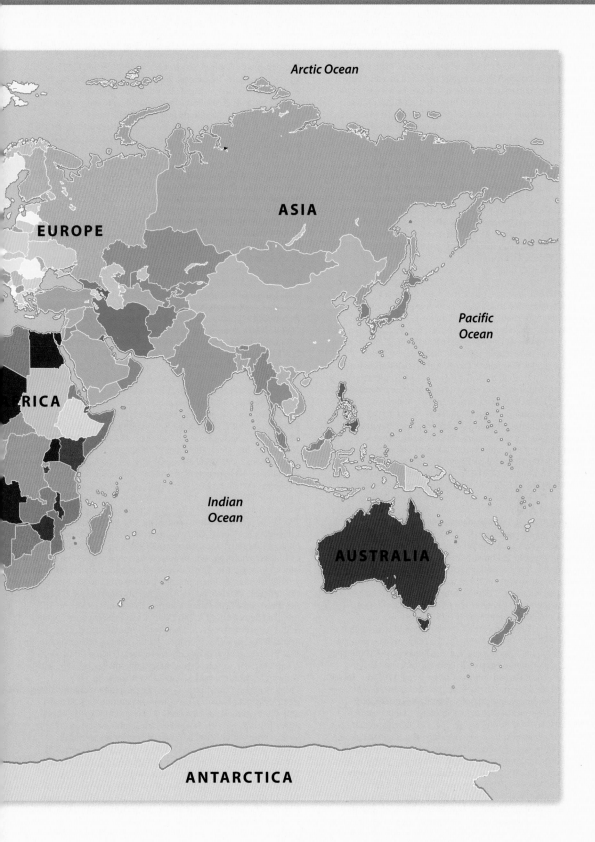

Arctic Ocean

ASIA

EUROPE

Pacific
Ocean

RICA

Indian
Ocean

AUSTRALIA

ANTARCTICA

shutterstock, Vitaly Maksimchuk/shutterstock, Imaginechina/ CORBIS; pg. 61: Arterra Picture Library/Alamy; pg. 62: Bill Pugliano/ Stringer/Getty Images News/Getty Images, Gene Krebs/istockphoto; pg. 63: Rolls Press/Popperfoto/Getty Images, Stock Connection Blue/ Alamy; pg. 64: North Wind Picture Archives/Alamy, Matthias Haas/ istockphoto, sjlocke/istockphoto; pg. 66: Ivy Close Images/Alamy; pg. 67: muratart/shutterstock, AFP/Getty Images/Newscom; pg. 68: Shu-Hung Liu/shutterstock, Stefano Bianchetti/CORBIS; pg. 69: Archive Images/Alamy; pg. 71: Adolf Ulrich Wertmuller/Collection: Bridgeman Art Library/Getty Images, Leemage /Universal Images Group/Getty Images; pg. 72: Big Cheese Photo LLC/Alamy, Pingebat/ istockphoto; pg. 73: North Wind Picture Archives/Alamy, Joshua Hodge Photography/istockphoto, Evgeny Bashta/istockphoto; pg. 75: Michael Kelley/Getty Images; pg. 77: Pawel Gaul/istockphoto; pg. 78 North Wind Picture Archives/Alamy, tomazl/istockphoto; pg. 79: Araldo de Luca/CORBIS, Anonymous/C-RMBett/AP Photo, IlonaBudzbon/istockphoto; pg. 80: Encyclopaedia Britannica/ Contributor/Universal Images Group/Getty Images, Visage/ Stockbyte/Getty Images; pg. 81: Hulton Archive/Getty Images, FPG/ Staff/Archive Photos/Getty Images; pg. 82: Wally McNamee/CORBIS, North Wind Picture Archives/Alamy; pg. 83: Patrick Frilet/Hemis/ CORBIS, Bettmann/CORBIS; pg. 84: Ocean/CORBIS, CORBIS; pg. 86: james boulette/istockphoto; pg. 87: AP Photo; pg. 88: North Wind Archives/AP Photo, gerenme/istockphoto; pg. 89: iofoto/ shutterstock, Education Images/UIG/Getty Images; pg. 90: www.loc. gov/pictures/item/cph6307/Library of Congress, monkeybusinessimages/istockphoto; pg. 91: Everett Collection Inc/ Alamy; pg. 92: AP Photo, Pablo Martinez Monsivais/AP Photo, Pablo Martinez Monsivais/AP Photo; pg. 93: CORBIS; pg. 94: Tish1/ shutterstock; pg. 96: Bettmann/CORBIS, Rubberball/Rubberball/ CORBIS; pg. 97: Warren K. Leffler/http://www.loc.gov/pictures/ item/2003688164/Library of Congress, Pablo Martinez Monsivais/AP Photo; pg. 98: Lebrecht Music and Arts Photo Library/Alamy, Tim Graham/Getty Images, Bettmann/CORBIS/AP Photo; pg. 99 NNehring/istockphoto, gerenme/istockphoto, Peter Newark Pictures/Bridgeman Art Library; pg. 100: olivier/shutterstock, gregobagel/istockphoto, mphillips007/istockphoto; pg. 101: lisafx/ istockphoto, Darin McGregor/AP Photo; pg. 102: leezsnow/ istockphoto, J.L. Kraemer/CORBIS; pg. 103: orderfinishedart/ istockphoto; pg. 104: Majid Saeedi/Stringer/Getty Images News/ Getty Images, Sjo/istockphoto, Paul Almasy/CORBIS, Dale Spartas/ CORBIS; pg. 106: North Wind Archives/AP Photos; pg. 108: Nataliya Hora/shutterstock; pg. 110: Bettmann/CORBIS, Libor Píška/ shutterstock; pg. 111: Bettmann/CORBIS, Oleksiy Mark/ shutterstock, Oleksiy Mark/shutterstock, Janfilip/shutterstock, pictafolio/istockphoto, Pakhnyushcha/shutterstock; pg. 112: Monkey Business Images/shutterstock, Mondadori Electa/ Bridgeman Art Library; pg. 113: BergmannD/istockphoto; pg. 114: anzeletti/istockphoto; pg. 115: NNehring/istockphoto, Chicago History Museum/Archive Photos/Getty Images, Joe Rosenthal/ CORBIS; pg. 116: Jim Bourg/Reuters/CORBIS, Jose Fusta Raga/ CORBIS; pg. 117: Pool Photograph/CORBIS, shcheglov/istockphoto, Bettmann/CORBIS/AP Photo, AP Photos/Texas Energy Museum; pg. 118: Gamma-Rapho/Getty Images, Tom Till/SuperStock/CORBIS; pg. 119: Arsgera/istockphoto, Warren K. Leffler/http://www.loc.gov/ pictures/item/2003688164/Library of Congress; pg. 120: Troy Aossey/ Getty Images, ZouZou/shutterstock; pg. 121: Bettmann/CORBIS; pg. 123: BrianBrownImages/istockphoto, Gamma-Keystone/Getty Images; pg. 124: RON EDMONDS/AP Photo; pg. 125: Bettmann/ CORBIS, SAUL LOEB/AFP/Getty Images; pg. 126: Bettmann/CORBIS, AP Photo, asiseeit/istockphoto; pg. 128: mico_images/istockphoto; pg. 130: dt03mbb/istockphoto, AdShooter/istockphoto; pg. 131: Louis S. Glanzman/Contributor/National Geographic/Getty Images; pg.132: Bettmann/CORBIS, Don Cravens/Contributor/Time & Life Pictures/Getty Images, LifeJourneys/istockphoto; pg. 133: PLANETOBSERVER/SCIENCE PHOTO LIBRARY; pg. 135: millraw/ istockphoto, moodboard/CORBIS, David Keith Jones/Images of

Africa Photobank/Alamy; pg. 136: AFP/Getty Images, The Art Gallery Collection/Alamy, PoodlesRock/CORBIS; pg. 137: kavram/ shutterstock, William Aiken Walker/Bridgeman Art Library/Getty Images; pg. 138: Terraxplorer/istockphoto, Elyse Lewin/ Photographer's Choice/Getty Images, ROBERT W. KELLEY/Time & Life Pictures/Getty Images; pg. 139: PhotoQuest/Contributor/ Archive Photos/Getty Images, Encyclopaedia Britannica/UIG/Getty Images; pg. 140: ZUMA Press, Inc./Alamy, tungtong/istockphoto; pg. 141: Hill Street Studios/Blend Images/CORBIS; pg. 142: SeanPavonePhoto/shutterstock, Ed Metz/shutterstock; pg. 143: JLP/ Jose L. Pelaez/CORBIS, 2009fotofriends/shutterstock; pg. 144: Everett Collection Inc/Alamy; pg. 145: DEA/G. DAGLI ORTI/Getty Images, CTR/AP Photo; pg. 147: Zhang Dacheng/Xinhua Press/ CORBIS, Komvell/shutterstock, Hulton-Deutsch Collection/CORBIS; pg. 148: pic4you/istockphoto; pg. 149: PhotoQuest/Contributor/ Archive Photos/Getty Images, Bettmann/CORBIS/AP Photo, http:// www.loc.gov/pictures/item/2003668413/Library of Congress; pg. 150: THONY BELIZAIRE/Staff/AFP/Getty Images; pg. 151: Matthew Ragen/searagen/istockphoto, Rahmo/shutterstock; pg. 152: MLB Photos/Getty Images, remik44992 /istockphoto; pg. 153: Ralph Crane/Contributor/Time & Life Pictures/Getty Images, Khomulo Anna/shutterstock, Evikka/shutterstock; pg. 154: Komar/ Shutterstock, Olga Lyubkina/og-vision/istockphoto; pg. 155: ISMIHAN OZGUVEN/ANATOLIAN AGENCY/epa/CORBIS, Mark Bowden /bowdenimages/istockphoto; pg. 156: Hemant Mehta /India Picture/CORBIS, Anna Kucherova/shutterstock, Image Source/ CORBIS, Tetra Images/Alamy, Bertrand Rieger/Hemis/CORBIS; pg. 157: Sergiy Serdyuk/ssuaphoto/istockphoto, Wally McNamee/ CORBIS, Hill Street Studios/Blend Images/CORBIS; pg. 158: Frank Tozier/Alamy, Klaus Leidorf/CORBIS; pg. 159: 13/Ocean/CORBIS, Steve Shepard/sshepard/istockphoto; pg. 160: oshun/istockphoto, PoodlesRock/CORBIS; pg. 161: Hill Street Studios/Blend Images/ CORBIS, Monkey Business Images/shutterstock.com; pg. 162: Tyler Olson/shutterstock; pg. 163: David Jones/istockphoto; pg. 164: Bettmann/CORBIS; pg. 165: Joe McDonald/CORBIS, Lynn Johnson/ National Geographic Society/CORBIS; pg. 167: Bettmann/CORBIS, ZUMA Pess, Inc./Alamy, Bettmann/CORBIS; pg. 168: Michael Reynolds/epa/CORBIS, AP Photo; pg. 169: monkeybusinessimages/ istockphoto, MPI/Stringer/Getty Images, American School/ Bridgeman Art Library/Getty Images; pg. 170: Underwood & Underwood/CORBIS; pg. 171: Burstein Collection/CORBIS, Bananaphoto/shutterstock, Dorling Kindersley/Getty Images; pg. 172: Luciano Mortula/shutterstock; pg. 173: William Aiken Walker/ Bridgeman Art Library/Getty Images; pg. 174: Richard Vogel/ photographer/AP Photo, Bettmann/CORBIS; pg. 175: Bettmann/ CORBIS/AP Photo; pg. 176: by Paul/shutterstock; pg. 177: sjlocke/ istockphoto; pg. 178: Troy Aossey/Getty Images, oriori/shutterstock; pg. 179: Monkey Business Images/shutterstock, Luciano Mortula/ shutterstock, CORBIS; pg. 180: Free Agents Limited/CORBIS; pg. 181: Art Directors & TRIP/Alamy, Matthew Cole/shutterstock; pg. 182: Archive Photos/Hulton Archive/Getty Images, Bettmann/CORBIS, Aelius Aaron/shutterstock, Axel Wolf/shutterstock; pg. 183: Brandon Bourdages/shutterstock, John Carnemolla/istockphoto; pg. 184: Hulton Archive/Stringer/Getty Images, Dorling Kindersley/ Alamy; pg. 185: Scott R Larsen/Flickr/Getty Images; pg. 186: Justin Sullivan/Staff/Getty Images News/Getty Images; pg. 187: ChinaFotoPress/Contributor/Getty Images; pg. 188: Charles Silvey/ mcsilvey/istockphoto; pg. 189: Chris Hill/shutterstock, Ricardo Alday/shutterstock; pg. 190: Boris Feoktistovich/Fine Art Images/ AGE fotostock; pg. 191: Songquan Deng/shutterstock; pg. 192: Staffan Widstrand/CORBIS, Universal History Archive/UIG/ Bridgeman Art Library; pg. 193: Eric Bechtold/Alamy, wdstock/ istockphoto, North Wind Picture Archives/Alamy; pg. 194: AP Photo; pg. 195: fstop123/istockphoto, 34/Ocean/CORBIS; pg. 196: Education Images/UIG/Getty Images, Pictorial Press Ltd/Alamy; pg. 197: YOMIURI SHIMBUN/AP Photo, H. B. Lindsley/photographer/ Library of Congress/http://www.loc.gov/pictures/item/2003674596,

Kurz & Allison/Popular Graphic Arts/http://www.loc.gov/pictures/ item/91482223/Library of Congress; pg. 198: Lebrecht Music and Arts Photo Library/Alamy, Bettmann/CORBIS, Bettmann/CORBIS; pg. 199: CORBIS; pg. 200: THONY BELIZAIRE/Staff/AFP/Getty Images, Gamma-Keystone/Getty Images, S.Borisov/Shutterstock, Henrik Winther Andersen/Shutterstock; pg. 201: Steve Froebe/istockphoto; pg. 202: Bettmann/CORBIS; pg. 203: jamesbenet/Getty Images, Robert Harding Picture Library Ltd/Alamy, Arterra Picture Library/ Alamy, Tim MacPherson/cultura/CORBIS, FPG/Staff/Getty Images; pg. 204: Rechitan Sorin/shutterstock, Bettmann/CORBIS/AP Photo; pg. 205: gerenme/istockphoto, Michael Tregenza/Private Collection/ Look and Learn/Bridgeman Art Library

Data Sources:

pg. 18: U.S. Census Bureau, *Income, Poverty and Health Insurance Coverage in the United States: 2011* (bias); pg. 21: Congressional Research Service/Library of Congress, *U.S. International Borders: Brief Facts* (border); pg. 28: U.S. Census Bureau, *1790 Census and 2010 Census: United States Profile* (census); pg. 31: U.S. Department of Homeland Security, *Annual Flow Report, U.S. Naturalizations: 2011* (citizen); pp. 31, 85: U.S. Census Bureau, *State and County QuickFacts* (city, income); pg. 42: StateofFlorida.com, *Florida Geography* (county); pg. 48: TreasuryDirect, *The Debt to the Penny and Who Holds It* (deficit); pg. 48: Apple, Inc., *Quarterly Results Reports, 2010-2012* (demand); pg. 49: Pew Research Center's Project for Excellence in Journalism, *State of the News Media annual report: 2010*, http://stateofthemedia. org/2010/network-tv-summary-essay/pbs/ (demographic); pg. 54: U.S. Census Bureau, *Employment, Work Experience, and Earnings by Age and Education: Civilian Noninstitutional Population: United States: Both Sexes* (earnings); pg. 55: U.S. Census Bureau, *School Enrollment in the United States: 2010* (education); pg. 61: CNN Money, *Your monthly gasoline bill: $368* (expense); pg. 62: U.S. Environmental Protection Agency, *Demographics* (farming); pg. 72: United States Holocaust Memorial Museum, *Jewish Population of Europe in 1945* (genocide); pg. 76: The World Bank, *GDP (current US$)* (gross domestic product); pg. 83: U.S. Department of Homeland Security, *2010 Yearbook of Immigration Statistics* (immigration); pg. 86: U.S. Government Printing Office, *Receipts by Source: 1934-2017* (income tax); pg. 92: National Archives, *Teaching With Documents: Documents and Photographs Related to Japanese Relocation During World War II* (internment); pg. 115: Encyclopedia Britannica: *Great Migration* (migration); pg. 141: U.S. Census Bureau, *State Totals: Vintage 2012* (population); pg. 142: New York City Department of City Planning, *Population Facts* (population density); pg. 205: U.S. Department of Labor, *Women in the Labor Force in 2010* (workforce)